# The Wind Shifts

# Camino del Sol

A Latina and Latino Literary Series

# The Wind Shifts

## New Latino Poetry

Edited by Francisco Aragón

Foreword by Juan Felipe Herrera

The University of Arizona Press   Tucson

recordando a mi hermana

# María Dolores Aragón

(1956–2004)

The University of Arizona Press
© 2007 The Arizona Board of Regents
All rights reserved

Library of Congress Cataloging-in-Publication Data
The wind shifts : new Latino poetry / edited by Francisco
Aragón ; foreword by Juan Felipe Herrera.
    p.  cm. — (Camino del sol)
    Includes bibliographical references.
    ISBN-13: 978-0-8165-2493-8 (pbk. : alk. paper)
    ISBN-10: 0-8165-2493-9 (pbk. : alk. paper)
    1. American poetry—Hispanic American authors.
2. Hispanic Americans—Poetry. I. Aragón, Francisco.
PS591.H58W56 2006
811'.54080868–dc22                    2006028665

Publication of this book is made possible in part by support
from the Institute for Scholarship in the Liberal Arts, College
of Arts and Letters, University of Notre Dame, and by the
proceeds of a permanent endowment created with the
assistance of a Challenge Grant from the National Endowment
for the Humanities, a federal agency.

Manufactured in the United States of America on acid-free,
archival-quality paper containing a minimum of 50% post-
consumer waste and processed chlorine free.

12  11  10  09  08  07    6  5  4  3  2  1

# Contents

## Richard Blanco

## Brenda Cárdenas

## Albino Carrillo

## Steven Cordova

## Adela Najarro

## Urayoán Noel

## Deborah Parédez

## Emmy Pérez

## Paul Martínez Pompa

# Foreword
## The Sweet Vortex of the Singers

> The bolero was composed for you and me.
> For all the ten year olds drawn
> to the plastic dials of the radio,
> drooling a bit perhaps,
> swaying uncontrollably as the air
> in the room tensed, focused
> on the sweet vortex of the singer's voice.
>
> —Lidia Torres (from "A Weakness for Boleros")

This new collection begins with Rosa Alcalá's *cante*, with deep-song, dream and the intersections of desire and reality, with a voice that flows as liquor and Flamenco drool, with meditative-talk and astute and hushed naked lines and a stiletto-shaped tongue; the orientations of the volume tilt toward the personal and the interior lives of lovers, daughters, mothers, *familias*, wanderers, healers, things, micro-moments, ghosts, shadows, and searchers. The voices here are angled carefully, an akimbo fusion of text and Latin@ word art, and on occasion the poems take a leap into macro-histories of conquest and colony, then delve down into "another part of the city," as one of Lidia Torres's poems mentions, a shadowy, slow-dancing place where existential lives flurry, sway, darken, blossom.

Francisco Aragón in his introduction notes how these writers set into motion various "expanding borders." He refers to the well-traversed poetics of "political" poetry, the verse of social change and civil rights *movimiento* poetry. In many ways this holds true; however, it seems that the powerful contributions here have more to do with the *contraction* of those supposed borders. We do not leap into a mega-politics or a supra-narrative of cosmic flux or power; on the contrary, here, in these twenty-five sections of poetry, we deepen into a *vortex* of micro-histories and herstories, we reverse the process of mitosis, past the nucleus and zygote, then rush into a María Luisa Bombal mist universe—meditations in umber, blanks, gaps, laminar surfaces. The *sensorium* of the verse seems paramount in this assemblage—what we read are sensory radiations of shapes, liquids, objects-for-themselves, jump-cut scenes, collisions of cultures, icons, memoria, body, texture, death, and danger. Here and there, a cunning guffaw erupts as in Urayoán Noel's metropolis of "Vegan power lunch grand slams!"—we reverb to a hip-hop rhythm riff *comedia* performance poem.

In some ways, this book is more than an expansion or a contraction, as Lidia Torres's poem "Blackout" suggests, the discourse here is one of a "congestion / of bodies,"—it is the lost cartography of an uncharted continent, adrift, shattered at the center, intersected by monumentalist histories of race, class, gender and sexual orientations, fictive memoirs, re-invented rituals, and "late capitalism." This is what makes this book vivid, electric, precise, and transgressive. Perhaps a more accurate or closer term or phrase for the new discourse in Latin@ poetry as sampled here is something that has to do with the engorged and blurred bodies, their *sound* of inner and inter-collision, that is, the "sweet vortex of the singers," as Torres expresses in her poem "A Weakness for Boleros."

The idea of music is central since the re-alignments and improvisations of line, rhythm, image, and space are key to each poet in this text. Poems go down, sideways, condense, blow out, suture, and elongate with dashes, caesurae, and asterisks. Latin@ calligraphy and palette-knife work is evident in every selection. The sweet vortex is designed and carved in various defiant and savory forms by each poet.

In this vortex of creation, congestion, and notation, many artists, writers, subjects, things, and places are in gestation: Darío, Madrid, Montale, Beijing, Apollinaire, and Cendrars make cameo appearances, juxtaposed with metros, Hamas, and Mediterranean tides and further navigations of the poet's speakers in fluid and borderless urban nations and cafés stumbling into loss and illuminations. Lorca rolls in wet and delirious and Nicaraguan. Terms repeat in *tumbao* rhythms, and pregnant fruit is sliced and devoured—bodegas, explosions, rooftops, and bullets. Prada, Gucci, and Havana drip into the body-flask, this abyss of letters.

What I love here is the sensorium, the pleasures of *memoria*, body, and experience. The smoky, hot, and fleshy canvas-work, the Kahlo brush, the Tamayo wash, the Siqueiros color sweep, all in some way or another, crashing and liquefying. A Latin@ Neo-Visual-Fauvism?

The vortex is hilarious, a party is on: *Cucarachas* at rave parties where Ginsberg's ghost spits mango rind on Cabeza de Vaca's portrait, there are numerous lovers in the house, sprawled in the dark, careless, without identities. As Aragón suggests, the question of identity belongs to a past generation of poets; this new clan seems to say it is more about the moment, or better yet, the furious fast-filters that grasp it, that tear it apart and taste it—as Brenda Cárdenas says in *"from* Sound Waves: A Series," "We feed. / Muscle is a buzzard's feast, / our brazos, his power to swarm." It is not identity, something whole, something that remains static and immobile that is at the center of the poem and the poet's tabula. Those things that rise and die are of more import—rain forests, sighs, and blurred silhouettes—and things close-up, zoom-lens of chileros in Las Cruces, Latin@ Kerouacs in low jeans grabbing train cars across the vestiges of an abandoned and collapsed nation, mouth agape at the stars and dark planets.

Therapists, TV jingles, and HIV. A car engine whirrs and the conversation fades, this is where "Mr. Dream" strolls into the scene. Personas, low-volume whispers, and muffled howls on Death, the big D cuts across the pages while we lay at the beach sipping Mojitos and listening to the latest alternative rock song on our iPod. Casual, dangerous, fleeting, alive, feeding through oozing texture and sunny withdrawal; this is the style, the Eros, the mood.

In our descent into the vortex, we become voyeurs of ourselves; we peek at a naked mother, listen to parents make love, we mention sperm and a crucifix in the embrace of five short lines as in Eduardo C. Corral's poem "Night Gives to Things the Turning Beauty of Leaves." This is the beat of the heat in this volume, stabbing-quick, so quick you feel the blood come down the skin—epochs after the assault or the ravenous bite. It is not about politics or movements or even aesthetics. It is what the aesthetics power—the acceleration of tension, intensity, collapsing surfaces, and mind-shift. When these four fuse and fission, the vortex blossoms song.

At times, we sense a scene or note a blurred clip of the past—the class analysis language of the Last Poets and the early Marxist Movimiento appears in the edge of a poem as in John Olivares Espinoza's "Aching Knees in Palm Springs." His poem says, "How I didn't care about dirt and weeds / From a bourgeoisie's garden." We hear the vernacular of plain-talk, which we then mambo into cucaracha shapes, stelae, and long line riffs, punctuated by the quixotic voice tradition and '70s poetic of the Chicano Bard of Dream-Walking, the magnificent Omar Luis Salinas, as in "I Go Dreaming, Raking Leaves." If you comb carefully, you'll find allusions to corporate Coca-Colas and other bad-colonial drinks, sundry items sounded out by Alurista in the early '70s and Carlos Fuentes in the '60s.

But don't grab the Cola because there are cameras and mosquitoes, departures and returns, homelands in between the exodus and the running, the always-runnings. Perhaps Gina Franco says it best in this wave of work; in "Velvet," she seems to point to the interior realm of the Vortex: a hyper-texture, a full immersion and dissolution of the body into the "Velvet," that is, the permeable "inside" of the displaced self or selves in motion and fragile transformations:

> But inside her, there is always velvet,
> velvet with its give and yield, the kind you
> find at a pet store, a bin full of long
> ears and noses busy snuffing up nerves
> among the cedar chips and their eyes
> opening wide as if rabbits couldn't know
> what softness brings . . .

Abuela herstories, Frida-blue hours and daffodils, hep talk and fine-cut passwords, boxing rings, Breton, béisbol, and Bacardí, that ol' time Cuban beverage named after the company once owned by one of Desi Arnaz's relatives before the Cuban revolution in the early 1900s—all here, whirling. The vortex spins, implodes, and rotates with the theory of the origin of the universe, Nirvana, suburban dogs with Elizabethan collars and forlorn telephone calls in Spanish, unanswered correspondences, letters and "sensations dissipating," as in Scott Inguito's poem "I Have Been Resisting, Due to Bad Knees, 'Falling into the Work of the Living'."

The material of the vortex is phenomenological, magical, mundane, studied, and guess-what, political: We touch Duende, crawdads, Juárez, *maquiladoras—and Plath*. Sheryl Luna adds the notion and sense of *dark paint*, the layered arc into the abyss, far from nationhood narratives of the Floricanto generation of the mid-sixties through the mid-seventies. The secretions of desire turn inward and dissolve, hydrate, disintegrate, then agglutinate, in some telluric, random, accidental, organic, and shamanic way, toward rebirth, unknowable in its process—in the vortex there are black holes and, most of all, mysteries without necessary deities. This is another nexus where this volume breaks ground. No longer do we reclaim ancestral religio-cultural figures, whether they are derived from Alurista's first three books, which served as cultural-poetic encyclopedias for many a poet, or Gloria Anzaldúa's ground-breaking work of the eighties, which opened the discourse of borderlands theory and poetics of self and spirit systems.

María Meléndez does conjure some of Anzaldúa's vision—one that sees into multiple selves and potencies of the spirit-woman. She speaks of wolf scents, wolf souls in between asterisks, and the Aztec Flesh goddess, Tonacacihuatl. What is brilliant with Meléndez as with the cadre of poets here is the search for the *unseen*, the topography of the minute—"Here's the turquoise cheek / of a fathead minnow . . ." María Meléndez writes in "An Illustrated Guide to Things Unseen." She is keen on the "laminar surface," the "feast of hidden droplets." More than, it seems, the formation of a new discourse, Melendéz's poetry points to a fresh Latina feminism.

The Cante by definition is dark. Yet it is a Wittgenstein "dark," a color-category-in-slippage, a black that emanates luminous properties—silence, gaps, stillness, water, waiting rooms, medications and pomegranates, chemotherapy and funerals and divorce, moist bodies and mother's high heels and satin bra, prosthetics, Speedos and Late Capitalism again, post-modern raps and blues, Rilke and Hopper, sawed-off braids, acequias, Sanskrit, and Durango belts.

Emmy Pérez, in her poem "La Aurora" speaks of "unidentifiable being." This, perhaps, is the clearest glimpse into the subject of the New Poetry Talk of the Latin@ Poet, if I can use capitals at all.

As bombs fly across once-nations, once-human figures, once-sustained ecologies and stable polities, once-respected demarcations, whether in the Middle East, London airports, or on the Latin@ Page of Verse, all borders and once-bordered figures are now, by all means and purposes, "unidentifiable." Here, in Aragón's diamond-eyed "expanded" selections, in these opened-Americas, all we have to hold on to, if at all, the 25 poets seem to say, is a "singing" in the vortex. Here, then, listen to its *bolero*, its velvet howl.

Juan Felipe Herrera
Tomás Rivera Endowed Chair
Department of Creative Writing
University of California, Riverside
August 2006

# Preface

Editing this book wasn't something I decided to do *one day*. Rather, it was the culmination of events that took place prior to the summer of 2004—when I assembled the sixty-page anthology proposal that I sent to the University of Arizona Press. In the interest of transparency, I offer the following to contextualize how the poets in *The Wind Shifts: New Latino Poetry* came to be included:

In the spring of 2000 I conceived of and founded Momotombo Press, a project whose initial mission was to publish chapbook-length collections by poets who hadn't yet come out with a book. Among the writers to appear in the first phase of the Press was María Meléndez.

Shortly after arriving at the University of Notre Dame in the fall of 2001 to pursue graduate work, I founded and went on to co-edit two issues of *Dánta: a poetry journal*. For issue number two, I edited a special section on emerging Latino/a poets. Through my conversations with noted writer Rigoberto González I learned of Eduardo C. Corral and Steven Cordova. Concurrently, a special issue of the *Indiana Review* brought to my attention Emmy Pérez. She, in turn, led me to Sheryl Luna. Writers Valerie Sayers and Richard Yañez spoke of Adela Najarro and Carolina Monsivais, respectively. Scott Inguito came into view when he initiated an e-mail correspondence with me. It was around then, as well, that I convened and moderated a conference panel on emerging Latino/a poets. Although I wasn't aware of it at the time, the foundation for *The Wind Shifts* was laid.

In the fall of 2003 I joined the Institute for Latino Studies (ILS) at Notre Dame. My first project was the Andrés Montoya Poetry Prize—a first-book award for Latino/a poets. As coordinator, I had the privilege of reading manuscripts from all over the United States in the winter of 2004. But even as I undertook that task, the idea of an anthology hadn't yet formed. If anything, I read those poets as potential Momotombo authors and not future contributors to this anthology. By then Momotombo had made its home at the ILS and honed its mission to publishing new Latino writers. Among the poets who submitted to the first edition of the prize were Kevin A. González, Paul Martínez Pompa, and Lidia Torres. The selection, therefore, of approximately half of the poets in this book was the direct result of the *professional* work I'd been doing in poetry editing since the spring of 2000.

Choosing the rest of the contributors involved research, which included noting who, for example, had been published in the Chicano Chapbook Series, who the University of Arizona Press had published in their Camino del Sol series, and who Wings Press in San Antonio had put into print. These sources yielded David Dominguez, John Olivares Espinoza, Carl Marcum, Albino Carrillo, Gina Franco, and Deborah Parédez. A look at a few anthologies, including March Abrazo Press's *Between the Heart and the Land: Latina Poets from the Midwest* and Martín Espada's *El Coro* produced Brenda Cárdenas, Venessa Maria Engel-Fuentes, and Naomi Ayala. Research on the Web led to Rosa Alcalá. Urayoán Noel I'd seen and heard perform at the Cornelia Street Café in Greenwich Village. I'd been reading the work of David Hernandez in various journals before I purchased his first book. And, finally, Richard Blanco's award-winning first collection had been a book I greatly admired.

Speaking of first books: that was the criterion for selection. At the time I put together the proposal, any Latino or Latina poet who had *no more* than one book in print and who was *approximately* forty years old or younger was eligible for inclusion. What I couldn't foresee was the pace of publication of any particular poet after the period in which I made the selection. In other words, I wasn't going to render ineligible any selected poet for getting a second book into print after 2004, as is the case with two of the poets here. Which brings us to the term "emerging." In some ways it's problematic because it suggests poets who have only recently started publishing, which isn't necessarily the case for some of the writers in this volume. Rather, the poets in *The Wind Shifts* belong to the generation of poets that follow those more established poets who were published in the major Latino/a anthologies of the nineteen nineties, or had more than one book in print—poets like Francisco X. Alarcón, Rane Arroyo, Jimmy Santiago Baca, Sandra M. Castillo, Lorna Dee Cervantes, Judith Ortiz Cofer, Victor Hernández Cruz, Silvia Curbelo, Martín Espada, Diana García, Ray Gonzalez, Maurice Kilwein Guevara, Juan Felipe Herrera, Valerie Martínez, Alberto Ríos, Aleida Rodríguez, Gary Soto, and Virgil Suárez.

Are there worthy poets who were eligible but who didn't make it into this anthology? Not surprisingly, yes. Factors such as limited space, timing, and, in one notable case, declining the invitation to be included, were the principal reasons. One might argue that more poets with shorter selections could have been an alternative route. But I decided, early on, that the model I wanted to follow was Ray Gonzalez's *Touching the Fire*, which included fifteen poets and generous samplings. On the other end of the spectrum was *Paper Dance*, an anthology that included fifty-five poets and three editors. *The Wind Shifts* aims for a middle ground at twenty-five poets with approximately ten manuscript pages of work for each contributor. I include as an appendix of sorts, however, a section titled "Further Reading" that lists some of the books whose authors could have been included in this volume but who, for the reasons mentioned, were not. A different editor may very well have edited a very different anthology. In the end, my hope is that readers seek out not only the books and chapbooks of the authors included here but also the books of the authors listed in this section just mentioned. *The Wind Shifts: New Latino Poetry* is but the first gesture of what I hope will be many, as was the case with the Latino poetry anthologies published at the end of the twentieth century.

F. A.

Dogs sprawl in the heat
tongues loll, drip saliva,
flanks ripple off flies.
The wind shifts.
I smell mesquite burning.

—Gloria Anzaldúa (from "Nopalitos," *Borderlands/La Frontera*)

# Introduction

In his introduction to *After Aztlan*, published in 1992, Ray Gonzalez wrote, when speaking of the contributing poets: "their voices share the common concerns of all Latino writers—finding ways to overcome political barriers placed upon them, [and] preserving the traditions of a culture that stresses close familial ties." Three years later, Victor Hernández Cruz, Leroy V. Quintana, and Virgil Suárez, in *Paper Dance*, emphasized a perspective that considers *all* of the Americas, underscoring that "the poets collected here are interested in language." Martín Espada, two years after that, in *El Coro*, an anthology of "Latino and Latina Poetry," began his introduction with: "The Latino community in the United States is clearly a community in social and economic crisis." And finally, in 1998 Ray Gonzalez once again, in presenting *Touching the Fire*, spoke of "[p]oetry by Mexican Americans, Puerto Ricans, and Cuban Americans" and how "the most effective manner of preserving the traditions of a culture, while evolving in a modern world at the same time, comes from the colorful language of daily experience." *The Wind Shifts: New Latino Poetry* echoes all of these concerns—and therefore recognizes, and is indebted to, these anthologies and the traditions from which they emerge. In other words, poems that address the social and the political continue to be vital strands in Latino poetry today. But if this focus, as underscored by Gonzalez and Espada, was the dominant mode in years past, the work in *The Wind Shifts* suggests that the canvas is now larger, its border expanded to include subject matter that is not overtly political. Rather, as suggested by Cruz and his co-editors, it is work that is equally, if not more, informed by an exploration of language and aesthetics.

Having said that, the vision that guides *The Wind Shifts* firmly recognizes that the bedrock of Latino poetry is Chicano poetry, both in proportion and subject matter. Chicano poets like Brenda Cárdenas, David Dominguez, John Olivares Espinoza, Carl Marcum, Carolina Monsivais, and Paul Martínez Pompa have elements in their work that concern themselves with the lives of the working class and, to some degree, sectors in our society that are on the margins. Consider these lines by Espinoza:

My mother pushes the grocery cart without a word,
Knowing that as newlyweds she begged outside markets for
    change
While Dad stole bread and sliced honey-ham inside.

*(from "Learning Economics at Gemco")*

Or these by Monsivais:

The name: I shuffle through faces until hers
becomes clear, jaw unhinged, skin covered
in grated ashy sores.

*(from "Phone Intake")*

On one level, given the topics—poverty, domestic violence—a poetics of witness is at work here, which is in line with the work one might associate with the origins of Latino poetry. But I must stress that regardless of the subjects taken on by the writers in *The Wind Shifts*, attention to craft is no less crucial as these two passages illustrate. The iambic rhythm in Espinoza's first line suggests a subtle nod to the traditions in English poetry. Monsivais, in her passage, makes deft use of internal rhyme with *name/faces* and slant rhyme with *hers/clear/sores*. In other words, even where the work addresses some of Latino poetry's common themes, attentiveness to language and sound is never sacrificed. With a poet like David Dominguez, the focus shifts from the working class, as in his poems about a sausage factory, to one that considers the life of the upwardly mobile—for instance, the experience of overseeing the construction of one's new home. But one can still detect an undercurrent of the social and the political here, as well. Dominguez does not avert his gaze when the speaker in one of his poems considers his situation—a Chicano who has, so to speak, "made it"—and presents this complicated scene:

At lunch, I go watch Mexicanos
who are putting the ceiling on my house.
They don't like me the moment
I park at the curb.
Extension cords crisscross the slab.
I nod at the fellow with the saw.

He's watching my feet,
nervous I'll trip and pull
the diamond-cut teeth
through skin, veins, and bones.
They have names for me: *pocho, gringo.*

*(from "Roof")*

But it would be an oversimplification to suggest that these poets write about these subjects in this way *only*. On the contrary, one of the arguments I would like to make is that the field of Latino poetry, where subject matter and aesthetics are concerned, has widened. And yet, I make this statement in full recognition that the principal lineage of this poetry is one that emerged from the social, political, and familial. And so Naomi Ayala, Kevin A. González, and Lidia Torres, who are Puerto Rican, or Venessa Maria Engel-Fuentes, who is of Bolivian descent, or Adela Najarro, who is of Nicaraguan origin, are represented here with poems that also take on these themes, primarily in narrative fashion.

Albino Carrillo, Gina Franco, María Meléndez, and Deborah Parédez are examples of poets in *The Wind Shifts*, who, I think, have begun to enlarge the parameters of Latino poetry in terms of newer perspectives on familiar themes, including such subjects as Huitzilopochtli, the Aztec god of the sun and war; the Spanish explorer Francisco Vásquez de Coronado; and life in the Southwest before the Civil Rights movement, to name just a few. Here is María Meléndez on Tonacacihuatl, the Aztec goddess:

How many spirits she's twin to, and how long she'll last in this
     world,
are secrets stashed in the rattle
of corn ears, in the coils
of venomous snakes.

Thirteen mirrors spangle her dress. For those sun-round
     mirrors,
praises are chanted by thirteen thousand red-legged hoppers.
At noon, she steps out of a culvert and collides with the naked
     light,
and her fever is an affliction known as August.

*(from "Tonacacihuatl: Lady of Our Flesh")*

One lens for Meléndez, then, is the flora and fauna of the natural world and what results when the human imagination, including our myths, interact with it.

Any discussion of Latino poetry, new or otherwise, would be incomplete without consideration of life on or around the U.S.–Mexico border. And while I don't mean to suggest, by grouping the following three poets around this theme, that their work is primarily informed by the border, it is, I believe, one of the concerns that surfaces in their poetry. Sheryl Luna, though she currently resides in Denver, grew up in El Paso, Texas. Eduardo C. Corral, who has a poem here titled "To a Mojado Who Died Crossing the Desert," is a native of Casa Grande, Arizona. And Emmy Pérez, a native of Southern California, makes her home in El Paso, Texas. The work of these three poets is intensely lyrical and influenced not only by place but by an extensive and intensive familiarity with the spectrum of contemporary American poetry, of which the poets in *The Wind Shifts* are a vital part. The poem that concludes Emmy Pérez's selection, "History of Silence," which is appearing in print here for the first time, is an example of a work that takes on a subject that is on the minds of many Latino/a artists—the unsolved murders of the women of Juárez—but it deploys a poetics that takes some of its cues from the more experimental tendencies in American poetry. Here is how the poem winds to a close:

A row of soldiers.
A row of bodies.
This is my row.
Definition: *Row:*
*Date: 1746*
: *a noisy disturbance or quarrel.*

Fresh corn rows
With silk tassels
I can be tender too
White and flattened
On a stone.
My sisters' bones.
Where are they?
Stalls in pupils

Between rows
In the desert
Dilating
Bullets
Mother
Corn
Utterance. History
Of indigenous.
The murdered women's pictures
Millions of self-portraits.

Luna, Corral, and Pérez are examples of artists who are very much interested in exploring the aesthetic boundaries of language and poetic expression, but who have not relinquished an intentional interest in what they write *about*, of which the U.S.–Mexico border is just one.

In attempting to sketch this "group portrait" by pairing particular poets with particular themes, whether they involve subject or form, I in no way mean to suggest that the poets in *The Wind Shifts* do not overlap or cross the artificial boundaries that anthology introductions like this one often present. Thus, it would not be completely accurate to say that the work of Richard Blanco and Francisco Aragón, for example, is informed *primarily* by the considerable traveling they have done outside of the United States—in Aragón's case, a ten-year residence in Spain. And yet I would venture to say that Blanco, a Cuban American, and Aragón, a Latino of Nicaraguan descent, emerge from that tradition of poets from the Americas—José Martí and Rubén Darío are two—for whom their time in Europe provided much fertile ground for their work. Blanco and Aragón do write about members of their families, as one might come to expect of Latino/a poets. But there is also what I will call a certain "nomadic" quality to their work, even as they write about specific places. Here, I think, is a passage in Blanco that is emblematic:

So much of my life spent like this—suspended,
moving toward unknown places and names or

returning to those I know, corresponding with
the paradox of crossing, being nowhere yet here,

leaning into the wind and light, uncertain of what

I might answer the woman to my right, anchored

in a flutter of cottons and leaning over the stern,
should she lift her eyes from the sea toward me

and ask: *So, where are you from?*
*(from "Crossing Boston Harbor")*

One of Steven Cordova's poems, like a number of Blanco's, is also set in Europe. "Meditations on the Jordaan" ends:

How you pedaled me past the Eerste Looiersdwarsstraat, right &
    east
    past three, four canals, left at the Singel.

How two days before departure there were three petals scattered
    about, two wilted flowers in the vase. One in full bloom.

Despite its northern European locale, the poem's manner and tone remind one of Frank O'Hara or James Schuyler, two poets often associated with the so-called New York School. A native of San Antonio, Texas, Cordova has made New York City his home for nearly twenty years. He is, I would argue, characteristic of the expanded terrain that Latino poetry now treads, evident in much of the work in this anthology—in Cordova's case, lyric poems that are intimate in their attention to the subject at hand, including, in this piece, the possibilities of love within the context of HIV. On the opposite coast, in Southern California, David Hernandez, like Cordova, writes skillfully crafted lyrics on a wide array of topics, including one yet to be discussed here, yet unavoidable when the subject is Latino poetry. "Dear Spanish" closes Hernandez's selection and it begins:

For kicking you in the shin in kindergarten
this is what I get: how to say good-bye
to my grandfather on the telephone

an hour before a plane shuttles him to Chile.

The poem, in addressing the speaker's complex relationship to the Spanish language, echoes Sheryl Luna's piece, "Learning to Speak," which ends:

*. . . Quiero*

*aprender español*, I whisper. He smiles. Blue hills
in the distance sharpen in an old elegance; the wind
hushes itself after howling the silences.

While Luna is forthright in expressing her ambivalent yet linguistically engaging relationship with the Spanish language, one of the poets in *The Wind Shifts* who is very much at home with it is Urayoán Noel. Born and raised in San Juan, Puerto Rico, but currently living in New York, Noel is not a Latino poet whose linguistic competence allows him to use Spanish words or phrases in interesting and relevant ways. Rather, Noel has outright command of traditional verse forms *in Spanish*, most notably the *décima*—the ten-syllable line employed in poems that have a set elaborate rhyme scheme. Here is a brief passage from "La lógica kool":

Filas de comunes fosas
en las ciudades antiguas,
sexualidades ambiguas,
fast food, fronteras porosas,
guerras de químicas rosas,
etnias que escurren rocío
y la utopía es un río
que vomita capital:
  *la lógica cultural*
  *del capitalismo tardío.*

This piece, in conjunction with its English version on the facing page, titled "Kool Logic" (or in a poem like "Barrio Speedwagon Blues") is indicative of how *completely* bilingual and inventive Urayoán Noel is. In deciding how he will present to English readers this title poem of his book, he does not, in my view, translate his poem. Rather, he *re-writes* it in English (it's his own poem, after all), using quatrains, while preserving rhyme as an important aesthetic element. So English readers read:

O.K. See the common graves
Rotting in the ancient cities?
The fast food? The porous borders?
The ambiguous sexualities?

The debt-bludgeoned ethnicities?
The wars of chemical roses?
Cash flows from Utopian rivers
And the market never closes!
    *"This is the kool logic*
    *Of late capitalism."*

What is particularly interesting about this work is that it employs traditional forms in ways that are refreshingly contemporary—where pop culture often takes center stage. One is reminded, in a way, of the English poet Thom Gunn's traditionally rhymed poems about taking LSD—dropping acid. Given the current demographic trends in the United States with immigration from Mexico, the Caribbean, and Central America, poetry like Urayoán Noel's poses the question: Might this be one future of Latino poetry? It would be a poetry where the Spanish language is not used to enhance the poem's aesthetic composition only, but rather a poetry where Spanish and English are on equal footing throughout.

Although it may not seem immediately obvious, the fact that the Spanish language enters into any discussion of Latino poetry takes us, ultimately, back to Spain. It is an interesting coincidence, therefore, that *The Wind Shifts*, which is arranged alphabetically, begins with a poet whose origins are from the Iberian peninsula. What is doubly interesting is that Rosa Alcalá's work seems to share affinities with some of the more avant-garde tendencies in American poetry. If "Cante Grande" represents, perhaps, Alcalá's less experimental side, as well as an homage to one of the more vibrant musical traditions from the south of Spain, "The Sixth Avenue Go-Go Lounge," with its generous use of white space, the short line or phrase, and the lack of an immediately recognizable narrative or plot, represents a facet of Latino poetry that remains underexplored and underappreciated within both the Latino literary community and the more established (read "academic") circles of the avant-garde.

Among the more vital regions in the United States, where poetry is concerned, the San Francisco/Bay Area has always been fertile territory. Scott Inguito, who is of Mexican descent, discovered his vocation as a poet at San Francisco State University, where he studied with D. A. Powell before pursuing his MFA at the Iowa Writers' Workshop. In "Guadalupe Beach," a poem set in a Mexican and Filipino community in

Santa Maria, California, Inguito takes on what has been one of the more prevalent domains of Latino poetry—family roots—but in a newer way. The poem begins:

> Say something
> Give me hymning
> If I have found my way
> Back to you
> On the floor
> At table
>
> The light line falls
> Your face
> If I have found
> Sing back to me
> In choirs of arms
> Faces wooden
> At table
> Bread is fondness torn
> Olives in the filling
> Grape-stuffed empanadas
> Pinched & curled
> With brown hands

Inguito's last selection in this anthology invokes Robert Duncan, the openly gay poet often associated with the San Francisco Renaissance and who, in American poetry, is a prime example of a literary artist whose influences were wide and variously rich. He was a poet whose admirers included more traditional figures like Thom Gunn on the one hand, and on the other, many of the poets who went on to be associated with the L=A=N=G=U=A=G=E school—perhaps the most developed of the experimental styles in the American literary avant-garde. Which is not to suggest that Inguito identifies himself as a Language poet. Like many of the poets in *The Wind Shifts*, when it comes to enriching and complicating their work, Inguito draws on the entire range of American poetry, including tendencies and styles one wouldn't initially associate with Latino poetry.

If Urayoán Noel's completely bilingual work represents one future for Latino poetry, work like Inguito's and Alcalá's might represent another—a poetry written by Latinos and Latinas who are very comfortable with deploying techniques and devices that resist and work against what might be called the more narrative or lyric traits most prevalent in Latino poetry up until now. Distinguished Chicana poet Lorna Dee Cervantes was once asked (I'm paraphrasing from memory here) the following question in reference to her piece, "Poem for a Young White Man Who Asked Me How I, an Intelligent, Well-Read Person, Could Believe in the War between the Races": "Why is this Chicana poetry?" To which she answered: "It's Chicana poetry because a Chicana wrote it." Cervantes's statement was useful then, and it continues to be useful today in the early twenty-first century. The "new Latino poetry," of which *The Wind Shifts* is but an initial sampling, is simply poetry written by Latinos and Latinas. Implicit in that assertion is a hard-won freedom—one whose origins include the first wave of the Chicano Chapbook Series in the late '70s in Northern California, in which Cervantes and Gary Soto played key roles. But equally important, I believe, were the efforts of Aleida Rodríguez in Southern California: between 1978 and 1984, she edited the literary journal *rara avis,* as well as titles for her small press, Books of a Feather. One of Rodríguez's aims was to provide a space for Latino and Latina writers whose concerns were more aesthetic than political. She was, in this sense, very much a pioneer—an antecedent to one of the principal claims of this anthology. Any attempt, therefore, to require or suggest certain aesthetic parameters, both in terms of subject matter and style, dishonors, I believe, the legacy of many of Latino and Chicano poetry's first adherents—both living and dead. A legacy, to be sure, that involved creating art informed by our community's stories and our social and political struggles, struggles that continue today, but which are also joined by a celebration, as well as an exploration of language.

Francisco Aragón
Institute for Latino Studies
University of Notre Dame
April 2006

Rosa Alcalá

## Cante Grande

> As if you could sing in the morning!
> —*Manuel Agujetas, Flamenco singer*

It's a dirty job
this voice of mine,
how songs insist
on my skin

they are well-traveled
clothes, not leaving
my body for days.
School children

carry books. I carry
memory, a gray
suit. What I offer
on good nights

are ashes and pictures,
things you've left
behind. What the hand
remembers might be

in it, a good meal,
any wine. My records
are no good.
They are morning

records. *El cante* needs
time to rise, to travel
the legs' length, to brush off
coal dust, to loosen

the throat's grip. *Cante* draws
on blood, houses cousins
from out of town, loses beds,
misplaces bets. Keeps faith

when evening shuts
in, when the heart shuts
down and is perfectly blind
to everything

but one face. How can it
come early?
A silversmith
for the tiniest bell

before dusk. Better yet,
ask the gardener
to drive away the scent
of violets. Songs might

never arrive. Either way,
somebody's going
to have to carry me
out. Then there will be

time enough to think
how every lemon grove
ends at your door, every
green pine offers

a view of your house.

## The Silversmith's Wife & the Chestnut Vendor

*Mi moreno*, stop pushing
your chestnuts past
my house. The fire you
sell draws this town's

pale branches. What if
my heart spills seeds.
What if the sleeping woke
early and caught the scent

of mint disturbed
in my backyard. It's been
so long since we've
seen an uprising

in the plaza, since
we've feared Moors.
Your bid reaches me
at the old wash banks,

and my hands turn
hot in water.

## Migration

In sleep, two unlikely
countries bordering

Bodies vigilant
to attack: at times

Axis, at times
Ally. Tonight we

lie awake, one hand
on each other's

gate. How far
to open it, how far

to slip through.
What casualty

will this bed
bring. Our chests idle

their tired patrol.
In confusion

we might smuggle
each other

past all regret.
And we are only

one foot into the other's
long walk home.

Which direction
to take:

forward or forfeit?

## Class

It's not work
just because
you can get it

It's the luck
of the hem
and the heel

a perfectly turned
drinking clause
made readable

What others call
internal dialogue
my dad would have called

brandy
It's not work
if you can spell

it. A union line
hemmed against
cold weather

gives Poles
and Spaniards
little to talk about:

pre-printed placards
struggle to rhyme
equality with anything

and Jersey
keeps me rubbernecking
like free verse

can cure
some poor fuck's
lung cancer

today, students
are working out
class schedules

so I propose
a course objective
of carrying paint drums

across the length
of my office
until someone gives

# The Sixth Avenue Go-Go Lounge

*(with thanks to Peter Ramos)*

breaks
      down
            the language
of sentiment

and the girl who
speaks
a fluent you
rubs
a little sense
into your lap

four bucks later
you think you've
made some progress—

subjectivity

finally *means* something


Outside
El Bombero wears a paper thin nightgown
once belonging to his wife

and tries to kill Paulie—
with an axe handle

*Can't blame*
*everything on*
*paint fumes*
*you little fuck*

You can't get up for this sort of thing *every* time

And cut rate
like blow jobs
behind
Union Dye
&
Frost Kwik
the Sixth Avenue Go-Go Lounge
is not
post industrial
post colonial
post modern

it's no sadder
than most things

it's not a text
to be *read*

(Hey
*No European Sports—*
READ
THE
SIGN.)

perhaps
dancer to drinker
ratio
suggests
the inflated
economy
of migration

or memory

*You cheap bastard*

Paulie, half-
blind
and
a smashed thumb
says

I can make you that
But it won't taste
like you remember


The Sixth Avenue Go-Go Lounge
making no apologies
for your future
problems,

Package Goods.
Open Christmas Day.


## Patria

*for José Alcalá García*

The salute
of this poem
rides open

to a shotgun—
I carry grief
as blatant

as propaganda.
My father's name
lifts

the hammer
bucket
brick

to eye
level
& makes everyone

a bit uneasy
for what's
to come:

a parched code
a cracked
body

's final test.
It's a Dallas
of suspicion

a ramshackle
conspiracy
of origins

that hides
a mother
so central

to the narrative
and fuses
time & again

melancholy to elegy
to bring the madre
patria back

to civil war.
This ditty
like Annabelle Lee

holds the beat
every foreigner
can tap his foot to

but whose feet
will be put
to the fire

for a democratic state?
When lost
in the sway

of our sorrow?
The flag
of our own names?

Francisco Aragón

# Café Central

*Plaza del Ángel, Madrid*

Of the three
      the one on his feet, a Dane—
slightly hunched, his arms loosely

      hugging, from behind, the hip-
shaped instrument of wood, his fingers
      punishing the strings picking

up speed as he grunts
      just audibly, the notes
of his solo

      within the piece, his forehead
near the rafters
      glistening . . . till he gives

the one from Catalonia
      at the keys
who can't see a thing

      in or out of those shades
a look, as if
      to say almost pleading *reel*

*me in!* So when finger and thumb
      strike—lighting the fuse—
both player and bass are pulled

      back down between piano
and drums, the three
      in the end hovering

safely near the ground again

*in memory of Tete Montoliu (1933–1997)*

## Lunch Break

Two hours between classes.
The short Metro ride home.
Coffee table, plates, glasses,

the TV flickering afternoon
news, sometimes a car-bomb . . .
And in the kitchen the singular tune

of his voice, his jokes, recounting this
or that—plot of a novel, book
he's put down, I bought for his

monthly fix (how he'd love
reading in the park what I took
half an hour to choose). Above

all, the sofa: digestion a nap,
my head nestled in his lap.

## Bridge over Strawberry Creek

"... à la belle étoile ... "

The path off the West Crescent that turns
briefly into the small
wooden bridge, and above it a canopy of leaves
—crossed and re-crossed

through the years, never pausing once for a peek
over the edge—the surface
blooming with concentric rings it's
beginning to rain

or water-striders skating around a stagnant
section of the creek.

And when I chose my place that morning
at the open window—redwoods

framed against June's day blue—it wasn't
the wind in the trees which
if I closed my eyes, had me on a balcony
in Sitges those summer nights

listening to the Mediterranean breathe
but rather the fact
of her voice, Madam Boucher's—meaning&sound
meshing in a phrase. I'm 12

and lying on a bed of chipped wood, warm
snug in the bag
facing the stars, my head sifting
the day: a morning hike, a dip

in the Russian River before lunch, before
the doorless stalls, the dank
cement on the soles of my feet, the towels,
the soap, the rich lather

lacing his chest


## Ernesto Cardenal in Berkeley

The books in my backpack
felt lighter walking
down the stairs at 24th & Mission: the sky
was clear and I wasn't heading for school . . .

Above, at the station's mouth, a preacher
wove Spanish while beyond him
on the ground a whiskered man
snored through the morning, his trousers

soiled. A thought flickered, swayed
(*Rubén Darío in Madrid* . . . ) as I rode
east along the floor
of the bay; commuters dozed,

later did crosswords going home, more
of them boarding at Embarcadero,
Montgomery, Powell. After
the reading I was a notebook

being filled—mamá y papá juntos a different
life billowing inside me:
a dusty street in Granada
or León, playing baseball;

or picturing in class how
Francisco Hernández de Córdoba
is led across the plaza he himself
had traced out with his sword,

beheaded

## Poem with Citations from the O.E.D.

First: *voz*   because I recall the taste
of beans wrapped in a corn
tortilla—someone brings it
to me, retrieves what's left
on the plate, the murmured vowels

taking root, taking hold—mi
lengua materna. Then later learn
another spelling, label the "box"
where sound's produced, draw, too,
the tongue, the teeth, the lips. *The voyce*

*that is dysposid to songe and melody*
*hath thyse proprytees: smalle,*

*subtyll, thicke, clere, sharpe . . .*
in thirteen ninety-eight. But what
of the deaf-mute, his winning shout

—BINGO!—knocking me over?
Huxley noted: *voice may exist*
*without speech and speech may exist*
*without voice.* The first time I spoke
with my father was on the phone, so his

was all I had to go on: that,
and what he'd say—things he'd hear
"inside." In *Doctor's Dilemma*
Shaw wrote: *When my patients*
*tell me they hear voices*

*I lock them up.* The pitch, the tone, the range:
a way of trying to know him. Now hers
and his are in the pages of a book:
*Un baile de máscaras* by Sergio
Ramírez, his characters echoing

words, rhythms I heard
until she died, hearing them as well
for months after—whenever I spoke
with him. *Who hath not shared that calm*
*so still and deep, The voiceless thought*

*which would not speak but weep.*


## Portrait with Lines of Montale

A patch of town-sick country

The old shop window shuttered and harmless
An odor of bruised melons oozes from the floor
Among wicker furniture and a mattress

Mildew like grass sprouts as well
The delicate capillaries of slime
Signs of quite another orbit

The ungraspable gorge
Sentiments and sediment
Where my carved name quivers

His laugh is jagged coughing

*for my father*

## Grid

> to write about a loved author
> would be to follow the trails he follows . . .
> —*Susan Howe*

—or Darío's Parisian phase
How during those winter
months he kept her
the shuttered flat
on rue San Michel
all-consuming flesh
his melancholy exile
Stood where Vallejo would
the melancholia of Darío
Vallejo    Between them
shared what they lacked
We track our own desire
that *soul-is-content* paradox
as in those lines that still
pulsing beneath the skin
*y no saber adonde vamos*
*ni de donde venimos*

———

Because they lived abroad
I was away for years
What meaning is there
in my head    their names
Free as oceans bottles
are what they are
another kind of mirror
material for a start
Consider all of this
an excursus on Origins
trace of the word *lugar*
I will inhabit a place
that doesn't exist
*Hay golpes en la vida*
*tan fuertes . . . Yo no sé*
Managua is Madrid

## Far Away

*(Rubén Darío)*

Ox I saw
as a child, breath
little clouds
of steam, vivid

in the sun, Nicaragua
a fertile ranch
abundant, rhythms
tropic, dove in a forest

of sound—wind,
bird, bull, ax:

the core
of me are these

and these I praise
yes, ox: lumbering
you evoke tender
dawn, the milking hour

when days were white
and rose, and you
cooing mountain
dove, recall

April   May
when spring
was all was
everything

## Al Viejo Mundo

Days I walked around swathes of you
Whose names slip my mind
I'm thirsty—come to me flowing
Down my throat: billboards posters
Doorplates twittering like parakeets
Through heaven came flying a thousand pigeons
I strode alone through your crowds
Buses in herds rolling by
I stood at the counters of your dirty bars
I ate in your restaurants at night
Often at long tables sharing a bottle of wine
Most mornings a milkman
Clinked glass along a lane
In the perpetual screeching of wheels
I heard a song
And my ears like taillights trail behind to hear it still

The great hearth of you with the intersecting
Embers of your streets—your old buildings
Leaning over them for warmth
And beneath: I rubbed elbows with your shuddering Metros
Some of them bellowing like bulls
The cry of their whistles could tear me apart
The skies above your plazas
Would turn deepening shades of violet
And your waves of traffic footsteps and the smell already
Of chestnuts roasting in a barrel on a corner
Your parks were lungs
Your air crisp enough to taste   sprinkled
With sputtering Vespas and horns
Your newly scrubbed
Neoclassic façades I loved looking at
And faces—faces glanced or gazed at
Waiting for lights to change
Once   not sidewalks but one   wide   walk—
Cars streaming up and down both sides of it
With merchant pavilions on my right and left:
News agents florists pet sellers and their chirping cages
Or descending stairs for a stroll behind a clear blue
Thundering sheet of water
And let me remember well the white-haired man
Descending ahead of us
Off the plane
How something in me fluttered hearing his vowels
Hearing in the sound of his voice
A message I'd take years to unravel as I venture
To inhabit once again your cities my self

*with Apollinaire and Cendrars*

Naomi Ayala

## Papo, Who'd Wanted to Be an Artist

Papo, lying on a Divine Street bench,
the divinity of neighborhood
angels kissing open his eyes.
Hymns, hymns for the angels
to whose work-beaten faces cling
the fishing nets of insomnia between the broken
bottles of missed hits at the numbers
store and the traffic going by. Papo,
he has small brown hands
that reach out from his eyes.
With them he smears the pollen
of *amapola* memories, dreams up an entire
town of angels, faces the color of the sun.
Amidst this flowering, he calls
for Ochún, her tight embrace. Ochún,
who has been in hiding. Once,
during a great experiment of will,
papo managed to pull silver
wings from Miguel's *costado*—
just before Miguel died. He had him flying
through smog, concrete, out to the air
bus he was always missing.
But Papo could not come along with him.
How was he to get back afterward?
Angels have such short life spans.
And, how was he to know?
That night, Ochún greeted him
with blood-red roses,
kissed his small weeping hands,
gave him moon
water from her breasts.
He was sure she'd come out this way again.
He had been waiting politely.

# It Was Late and She Was Climbing

It was late & she was climbing
up the hill with her babies,
late and he climbing onto her—
her belly glowing fire.
She climbed the steps of the day
with all she could carry
& the day climbed onto her, too
& they rolled together until night broke
them into pieces they looked
for in the morning.
Everywhere light
spilled out from her belly.
It doubled with every touch.
This went on for a long time
until everything around her became light.
Late & no matter how early,
dawn sometimes,
she went on blinding birds
& men & children
& women showed up to her house wearing visors
& she had to hug every thing & everyone
to grow small enough
to fit into her climbing.

# This Breathless Minute

Our blood runs free forever before we ever
do. Do this, do that, but our blood glides
smoothly the way we sometimes wish
we could—over concrete, past the screeching
wheels of patrol cars, stunning the whiteness
of emergency after emergency come
a little too late. I am sick

to breathlessness. My body's sick. I
got the cancer you get from the spell
spilled blood casts on you. Everywhere I look
blood brands a house front, draws a line
of impermanence across a child's butterflied belly—
no growing down into her bones
before she gets that glimpse
of the bridge across, a bridge we think is sturdy
and will hold out walking. I am trying to stay
inside this country. I am trying very hard
to stay inside this country—today, this afternoon,
this breathless minute, but everybody's blood
is mixed into the blood that runs through here
and I can't tell my left foot
from my right hand.

## My Brother Pito

My voice, when I ache for his
is the steering
wheel of a car under my fingers
in wintertime
before the car warms up.

His voice
a voice whose words I rummage
through like a dresser drawer
where everything falls in and away
and is bound
to show up somewhere sometime.

Voice of *naranja dulce* and
*limón partido* . . .
Voice of give and embrace.

Voice like train tracks
fade into the skyline,
into a fine nowhere I never
get to see long enough to
follow the wind.

Palm leaf, ripe mango skin voice,
he gives to me a joy
of spirit like coconut
water in desert heat, enough
for me, enough to pass around.

## For "S"

If a green leaf is no more alive to you
than your toe is without you
then go on about your life
flattening soda pop
cans for a pastime
leaning against the concrete
walls of shopping plazas
or gray corporate buildings waiting
on some cash to rain down
leaning against the soft side
of a woman trying hard to be gentle & alive
you can watch t.v.
tan in its technicolor splendor
though maybe
a toe's better off without you
sure it could feed something
sometime
or some new thing
shoot out from it like huckleberry
from a dead tree

# Hole

One morning they dig up the sidewalk and leave.
No sign of the truck,
only the large
dark shadow digging and digging,
piling up sludge with a hand shovel
beside the only tree.
Two o'clock I come by
and he's slumbering in the grass beside rat holes.
Three and he's stretched across a jagged stone wall,
folded hands tucked beneath one ear,
a beautiful young boy smiling,
not the heavy large shadow who can't breathe.
Four-thirty and the August heat
takes one down here.
He's pulled up an elbow joint
some three feet round.
At seven I head home for the night,
pass the fresh gravel mound,
a soft footprint near the manhole
like the "x" *abuelo* would place beside his name
all the years he couldn't write.

# Within Me

War begins right here on my street.
It begins with me.
I see her weapons in the eyes of a child,
her face on windowpanes.
There are times I want war.
I lie down with her.

I stroke her back.
There are times she enters my house
and I enter into battle with her.
War slips in, into my name.
I have her in my blood.
She sweetens my morning coffee on Saturdays.
I betray her. I hide from her. I run away
but already war knows the course of my dreams
and wants to steal the children of my soul.
War begins with me.
It is with me that war begins
right here on my street
in the small showers of bullets
in an empty garbage can
in what I say and do not say
in the bewitching ivy of tedium
in the soap I use to bathe.
She is in my fingers
in the shadow of my eyes
in my lover's hair.
I sing to her so that she may leave
so that war leaves me.
Today I sing to her
and she lets me sing.

## Thus

At six the glass roses would be watered.
At six the tomatoes and lima beans.
At seven the machete would be sharpened.
At the forcible hour, the groan of the moon
swelling in women's bellies.
At that hour in which the crow would kneel
on the shoulders of the ripened breadfruit.
At nine the return to coffee,

the tip of the chin sweating its scent.
At nine the noontime sun would be lying.
At twelve, nine perishing.
At one Eve's rib would suffer
the weight of the man it held up.
From the body, wheat ears sprouting.
The viand loosening from the iron pot,
the cassava would fight the *yautía*,
the sweet banana make a scene.
At two love was a mirror,
watching the cane fields from the corner of its eye,
hurling the bait of its breath,
forgiving mornings predictable as catch.
At four, four would become a gag.
At five, five would explode.
At six the bread would bless itself
and the dishes wash themselves alone.
At seven, the porch and the hammock,
the night a country without borders,
without muddled languages.
Mute as the rooftops
the spirits guarding their turn.

## Griot

Saturday adrift
on the wings of a strange bird
shrieking Spanish.

Blue smoke in the cold air
beneath helicopters, real
cliff-hangers.

He spins bodega loves
come and gone,
low-down addictions,

who got turned back
from the not so pearly gates
only to suffer more.

He could graffiti a poem
back of the only bus here
if only it would come to him,
if only he could make it
through the muttering wind.

## Horses

I don't know shit about horses.
I only see them in some of the dogs
that walk through here.
See them in the bear I've seen at the zoo.
Dark is all these things that
remind me of horses.
Dark like the wind
against the street with its lightbulb eyes.
Dark like you own the ground
and your own running.
This is the year of my horses.
They leap from my skin
and let loose on the block.
Bare back.
This is the year.
I speak horse with my skin
and own the language of hoofs hitting the ground.
My wind and my way out.
I came with horses into this dark
of no wind.
Prepared and unprepared.

Richard Blanco

# Mother Picking Produce

She scratches the oranges then smells the peel,
presses an avocado just enough to judge its ripeness,
polishes the Macintoshes searching for bruises.

She selects with hands that have thickened, fingers
that have swollen with history around the white gold
of a wedding ring she now wears as a widow.

Unlike the archived photos of young, slender digits
captive around black and white orange blossoms,
her spotted hands now reaching into the colors.

I see all the folklore of her childhood, the fields,
the fruit she once picked from the very tree,
the wiry roots she pulled out of the very ground.

And now, among the collapsed boxes of yucca,
through crumbling pyramids of golden mangos,
she moves with the same instinct and skill.

This is how she survives death and her son,
on these humble duties that will never change,
on those habits of living which keep a life a life.

She holds up red grapes to ask me what I think,
and what I think is this, a new poem about her—
the grapes look like dusty rubies in her hands,

what I say is this: *they look sweet, very sweet.*

# Shaving

I am not shaving, I'm writing about it.
And I conjure the most elaborate idea—
how my beard is a creation of silent labor
like ocean steam rising to form clouds,

or the bloom of spiderwebs each morning;
the discrete mystery how whiskers grow,
like the drink roses take from the vase,
or the fall of fresh rain, becoming
a river, and then rain again, so silently.
I think of all these slow and silent forces
and how quietly my father's life passed us by.

I think of those mornings, when I am shaving,
and remember him in a masquerade of foam, then,
as if it was his beard I took the blade to,
the memory of him in tiny snips of black whiskers
swirling in the drain—dead pieces of the self
from the face that never taught me how to shave.
His legacy of whiskers that grow like black seeds
sown over my cheek and chin, my own flesh.

I am not shaving, but I will tell you about the mornings
with a full beard and the blade in my hand,
when my eyes don't recognize themselves
in a mirror echoed with a hundred faces
I have washed and shaved—it is in that split second,
when perhaps the roses drink and the clouds form,
when perhaps the spider spins and rain transforms,
that I most understand the invisibility of life
and the intensity of vanishing, like steam
at the slick edges of the mirror, without a trace.

## Varadero en Alba

i.     *ven*

           *tus olas roncas murmuran entre ellas*
             *las luciérnagas se han cansado*
               *las gaviotas esperan como ansiosas reinas*

We gypsy through the island's north ridge
ripe with villages cradled in cane and palms,

the raw harmony of fireflies circling about
amber faces like dewed fruit in the dawn;

the sun belongs here, it returns like a soldier
loyal to the land, the leaves turn to its victory,
a palomino rustles its mane in blooming light.
I have no other vision of this tapestry.

**ii.**     *ven*

> *tus palmas viudas quieren su danzón*
> > *y las nubes se mueven inquietas como gitanas,*
> > > *adivina la magia encerrada del caracol*

The morning pallor blurs these lines:
horizon with shore, mountain with road;
the shells conceal their chalky magic,
the dunes' shadows lengthen and grow;

I too belong here, sun, and my father
who always spoke paradise of the same sand
I now impress barefoot on a shore I've known
only as a voice held like water in my hands.

**iii.**     *ven*

> *las estrellas pestañosas tienen sueño*
> > *en la arena, he grabado tu nombre,*
> > > *en la orilla, he clavado mi remo*

There are names chiseled in the ivory sand,
striped fish that slip through my fingers
like wet and cool ghosts among the coral,
a warm rising light, a vertigo that lingers;

I wade in the salt and timed waves,
facing the losses I must understand,
staked oars crucifixed on the shore.
Why are we nothing without this land?

# Chilo's Daughters Sing for Me in Cuba

They folded and shaped each banana leaf
like a paper flower with their calloused fingers
to make the tamales, filled with thirty ears
of cornmeal ground by hand. They helped
Ramon with the slaughter yesterday, seasoned
the pork overnight with salt, cumin, bay leaves.
They culled through every grain of wild rice
and every pound of black beans they could buy
on the black market. They sold three months
of soap rations for a string of garlic, crushed
the garlic, had enough olive oil to make *mojito*
from the *yuca*. They pulled the *yuca* from the soil
of their father's field this afternoon—washed it,
cut it, boiled it—until its heart bloomed open,
tender and white as its flower. They prepared
jugs of watermelon *refresco* and set the table
for twenty with borrowed plates and tin cups—
but no napkins. Now, they serve their dishes,
stand around us, and begin singing a cappella
for me, glad I've come to see them again, to sit
at their table, eat what their hands have made,
listen to their songs. Rosita sings old boleros
for our *tíos* and *tías* still in love with love.
Nivia sings *danzones* to honor our grandfathers
who'll be buried in the same ground they tilled.
Delia sings the old *décima* verses of *guajiros*
who made poetry out of cutting sugarcane.
And we all sing *Guantanamera*, over and over
again—*Guantanamera* because today the food
is plentiful, the earth continues to give them
what they need—*Guantanamera* for the lyrics
that praise the good people of this country
where the palms grow—*guajira Guantanamera*
because the revolution that never ends will
never change them, their stories, this land.

# What Is Not Mine

I wake to find you've left, and left a note: *Please*
*wait for me, I'll be right back* scribbled over the seal
of an envelope with your key, just in case I want
to leave your home that I've borrowed two days.
I don't know where anything is or belongs, only
that it is exactly January in the windows, as I wait,
a thing among the stillness of things that are not
mine: the upside-down cups I haven't drunk from,
stacks of plates like faces I've never met, the ferns
I've never watered, books in rows like an audience
that has watched us undress, the sheets iced over
your bed, a bud vase on your nightstand, next to
the black hands of a clock like mime gesturing
an end to our time together. I'll leave, leaving only
the swipe of my hand over the bathroom mirror,
whiskers on a razor, a mug of thickened coffee,
traces of my cologne and cigarettes on a pillow.
And my only defense will be that I must return
to what's mine, not wanting to, but having to
become who I was, before I was here, unsure
of just how the bare branches can bear winter.

# Crossing Boston Harbor

The horn blares—once—twice—sounding like
iron, a dull and heavy slap across the wind's face.

And if the wind could have a face, it would resemble
these strangers, blank as paper dolls propped up

against the railing as the propeller torque vibrates
through the vessel, slowly peeling the hull away

from the barnacled dock, the limp ropes coiled
like dry roses on the metal deck, the anchor up

like a rusty bow hung on the bow, and we move
all together, at the same speed, to the same point.

The ferry's chine makes an incision across the bay,
its churned waters bleed a wake of lustrous blue

behind us as we head west, scanning the coastline
nested with gables and fringed with flocks of sails,

their peaks waning out of sight into memory, until
there's nothing left to measure my distance against.

So much of my life spent like this—suspended,
moving toward unknown places and names or

returning to those I know, corresponding with
the paradox of crossing, being nowhere yet here,

leaning into the wind and light, uncertain of what
I might answer the woman to my right, anchored

in a flutter of cottons and leaning over the stern,
should she lift her eyes from the sea toward me

and ask: *So, where are you from?*


## Mexican Almuerzo in New England

*for M.G.*

Word is praise for Marina, up past 3:00 a.m. the night before her flight,
preparing and packing the *platos tradicionales* she's now heating up
in the oven while the *tortillas* steam like full moons on the stovetop.
Dish by dish she tries to recreate Mexico in her son's New England
kitchen, taste-testing *el mole* from the pot, stirring everything: *el*

*chorizo-con-papas, el picadillo, el guacamole.* The spirals of her stirs match the spirals in her eyes, the scented steam coils around her like incense, suffusing the air with her folklore. She loves Alfredo, as she loves all her sons, as she loves all things: *seashells, cacti, plumes, artichokes.* Her hand waves us to circle around the kitchen island, where she demonstrates how to fold tacos for the *gringo* guests, explaining what is *hot* and what is *not*, trying to describe tastes with English words she cannot savor. As we eat, she apologizes: *not as good as at home, pero bueno* . . . It is the best she can do in this strange kitchen which Sele has tried to disguise with *papel picado* banners of colored tissue paper displaying our names in piñata pink, maíz yellow, and Guadalupe green—strung across the lintels of the patio filled with talk of an early spring and *do you remember*s that leave an after-taste even the *flan* and *café negro* don't cleanse. Marina has finished. She sleeps in the guest room while Alfredo's paintings confess in the living room, while the papier-mâché skeletons giggle on the shelves, and shadows lean on the porch with rain about to fall. Tomorrow our names will be taken down and Marina will leave with her empty clay pots, feeling as she feels all things: *velvet, branches, honey, stones.* Feeling what we all feel: home is a forgotten recipe, a spice we can find nowhere, a taste we can never reproduce, exactly.

## Time as Art in The Eternal City

The first shadows appear like cells slowly dividing
from every tree and lamppost while my first words
divide from me onto my journal, trying to capture
how dawn light melts over the city's blank windows
and its ancient doors, opened a thousand-thousand
mornings to the sun with questions, and closed
on the moon's face without answers. All the days
that have fallen through these courtyards and alleys,
the lives that have worn these cobblestones gray,
all the gray doves that have been cast into flight
by how many church bells? After all the centuries

that have been tolled, hour by hour, and disappeared
above these domes, can it matter that I'm here now:
watching the bougainvillea blaze over the terraces,
counting on the morning to dive into the fountains,
flicker over coins, light the water up with my wishes?
Today, a temple will lose yet another stone that will
continue being a stone, and the Colosseum will move
again through its own shadow. Today, the murdered
and murderers will be remembered and forgotten,
and an empire pardoned for the sake of its beauty
in this city where time is an art. Today, a tourist
once again sits at a café with an espresso, a pen,
waiting to enter the Pantheon, waiting to gaze up
into its oculus, opening like a moonful of sunlight
in its dome, ready to stand in that beam of light,
to feel something radiant, and write it down.

## In Defense of Livorno

The dove-white hull glides into port just after sunrise. We rise to a
hum vibrating from the engine room up to our bunks nine decks above
the sea, expecting something postcard-ish in the porthole, something
very Italian, very Mediterranean. Perhaps an arc of mountains dotted
with villas, a legion of sailboat masts at bay, or a harbor of weathered
rowboats bobbing on a quilt of seawater greens. Not this sea of blue,
yellow, and red freight cars stacked like toy blocks, not the blotches
of oil on the docks, not the acrid grind and burn of diesel engines. At
breakfast, from behind tiny glasses of orange juice and porcelain cups
of coffee, everyone's eyes are asking: *Where the hell are we?* We're in
Livorno, but we're not supposed to see it; we're supposed to herd off
the ship into a bus, maneuver through a labyrinth of cargo, ignore the
miles of sea wall, and get out of Livorno. We're supposed to pity its
empty beaches and bombed-out villas, then cross through the wine and
cheese of Tuscany to arrive at Pisa, where we're supposed to follow
our guide's orange flag as he marvels over the miscalculation, listen to

his reverent whispers lead us through yet another cathedral, to goggle over altars and paintings commissioned with alms. We're supposed to lap up gelato, buy Tower-of-Pisa ashtrays, then skip to Florence where we're supposed to revere the Medici, as we stroll through *their* palazzos, pausing at *their* paintings to say *hmm* and *wow* and *isn't that amazing*. We're supposed to buy Prada shoes and Gucci belts, get tickets to see David, pretend not to notice his penis, then get back on our bus, awed by the brilliance of humanity, satisfied by beauty all the way to Livorno. We're not supposed to need Livorno: its barrels of oil and pallets of Chianti, its pounds of prosciutto and cans of coffee, its tons of sugar and made-in-China trinkets. We're not supposed to see anything beautiful here, not even the names glazed over the boxcars—Delmas, Yan-Ming, Haypag, Maruba, Cronos, Masto, Maruba—craned through the sky like new words from the gods, arriving from the very heavens.

## Somewhere to Paris

> The sole cause of a man's unhappiness is that he
> does not know how to stay quietly in his room.
> —*Pascal,* Pensées

The *vias* of Italy turn to memory with each turn
and clack of the train's wheels, with every stitch
of track we leave behind, the *duomos* return again
to my imagination, already imagining Paris—
a fantasy of lights and marble that may end
when the train stops at *Gare de l'Est* and I step
into the daylight. In this space between cities,
between the dreamed and the dreaming, there is
no map—no legend, no ancient street names
or arrows to follow, no red dot assuring me:
*you are here*—and no place else. If I don't know
where I am, then I am only these heartbeats,
my breaths, the mountains rising and falling
like a wave scrolling across the train's window.

I am alone with the moon on its path, staring
like a blank page, sheer and white as the snow
on the peaks echoing back its light. I am this
solitude, never more beautiful, the arc of space
I travel through for a few hours, touching
nothing and keeping nothing, with nothing
to deny the night, the dark pines pointing
to the stars, this life, always moving and still.

# Brenda Cárdenas

# Empty Spaces

She is a switchblade afraid of the hint in a two-second glint that might spring you an arm's length away. *I fear.* She kisses close, to shut the open gate of hunger, heavy-footed as history perched on her chest. *Empty spaces.* She never rests. Stumbling through the clutter of language, she rummages cramped closets for her lost sounds—igriegas y erres—tumbling like marbles spilled in the attic. *Spaces I fear.* She mainlines white noise—a guest persistent as rain flooding her muted room. *Spaces.* She adds another hue to the walls crawling with orange and blue that zigzag the curves of her world to the ceiling. *I fear empty spaces.* She is reeling in a ravenous subjunctive that would doubt its own bones were it not for her grip slipping from your moist shoulders to the winter of metal bedposts. *Spaces I empty.* She grinds against you, minding only the bland blue sky that filters through the O'Keeffe hollow of her pelvis. *I empty fear.* In this abyss, she comes, braying the silence away.


# Report from the Temple of Confessions in Old Chicano English

*(after an installation by Guillermo Gomez-Peña and Roberto Sifuentes)*

Se cruzan canyons        en el templo de confessions.
Language lies        across the barbed lines,
piles of its limbs        pierced y pinchados.
Risky recordings        reveal what we think
of the Other        offering his objectified body
to the river rats        who ride his wetback,
the coro de coyotes        who crave his flesh,
the whey-faced who        whisper their sin in his ear,
the translators who trap        and trade his tongue,
la raza who receive him,        la raza who repel him.

In this chamber the chill        of chicken flesh—
pollito mojado        picoso y picado,
the black body        bag of the repatriated.
Here the distorted words        of debutants y do-gooders,
of know-no-betters        y neo-Nazis,
of Beowulfs and other        born-again beasts,

of sandaled sombreros      sleeping under cacti,
of Machiavellian     mentes y mouths
of anthropological     autoethnography,
of pretend pachucas     peeling their layers,
of preachers and poets     with puckered lips
of the misused multi-     cultural machinery,
of the Hispanic hodgepodge     hiding their Indio,
of the Quetzalcoatls     concealing their conqueror
de la migra meando     marking its turf.

Here, the hemistiched     hemispheres blend,
a vacuum of voices     absorbed in the velvet
paintings of slick     y sexy santos,
of the Aztec icon     at the altar of Aztlán
tripping and turning     transvestite warrior,
of the cyber-cholo     stripping down—Simón!
The vato loco's liquid     eye lures us
over borders, their blurred     tumbling barriers,
calling us to come     stare into the cage—
jaula de joda     aquí juntándonos—
the table turned     and tacked to the wall,
lit with votives     licking our luscious
breakfast bowl     of cucarachas on their backs
squirming to free     their feet and fly.

## Cartoon Coyote Goes Po-Mo

Coyote, he never learned the high concept.
He's still rapping at rave parties,
skate-boarding under deconstruction,
past computer networks
(keeps his Olivetti electric in the closet).
Everyone wonders when he'll catch up
like his sister, the computer-hacking CEO
of a major pharmaceutical company.
Baby, hers are smart drugs—
performance art provocateurs
tricking the tricksters,
not the white heat Coyote shoots, snorts, swallows.

*Hey honey, I can fly*
*through Ginsberg's naked streets at dawn.*
Coyote, he don't quite get it,
applies queer theory to his reading
of Burroughs riding freight train.
In a post-structuralist world
you ride on top of the axles
underneath either end of a boxcar
and watch the sparks fly!
*Don't get a cinder in your eye.*
That's the cyberpunk way to get
your mojado butt from the frontera
to the fields or the service sweatshops.
Only if coyote don't find you first,
and if he does, he'll eat you alive,
crunch you down like chicharrón
because he don't want no
vegan dietary restrictions;
no one gonna lay that trip on him.
He'd rather gorge himself on your sweet meat
until he auto-deconstructs,
blows himself to bits
all up and down the Rio Grande.
And in the time it takes you to find
his plastic voodoo in your Lucky Charms,
he'll be warming a stool in the cantina
at the next border town.
How's that for signification theory?

## *from* Sound Waves: A Series

> The river on the other side
> of English is carrying the message
> —*Víctor Hernández Cruz*

Tono—*D*

Some days cushion the dental edges
of our lives like night's cool curve

swerving into the music of light
dándonos the soft shoulder de voz.

Danilo y Diana sweep the street
of its blossoms, dejan piles
of magenta petals lining the gutters
de la colonia. Sí, hay basura,
un cigarillo acá, una lata allá,
but we are blinded by hyacinth
suns bursting from the pavement.

When dusk sinks into la plaza
desliando our braided days,
one hundred black wings
sing in the ceiling of leaves
above Gabo's favorite cafe,
the curl of *carru carru carru*
floating like a feather to his chair.

This day es una danza de dedos
pressing half moons into clay,
the consonant touch of tongue
to teeth arching the sound away.

Duración—*V*

> *Aquí vuelan aves arracimadas como uvas*
Clusters perch over
open-mouthed stones,
the sculpted men arcing back,
necks straining toward gods and vines,
elbows raised in angles.
Birds veil the starved sun.

> *Aquí vuelan aves arracimadas*
This is the *V* in Cabeza de Vaca
sweating the salt of the bay
in a migration that halts and hovers.
Is it the glint of obsidian that lures
vultures to the eye of earth?
Or jade of stone beasts that pull

thieves up the open-legged vertices
of our pyramids? We vanish

    *Aquí vuelan aves*
in the wind-worn skull of the long-
horn, in mutations making bowls
of eye sockets, cups of its keratin.
We carve hilts for our bowies
from the open jaw. We feed.
Muscle is a buzzard's feast,
our brazos his power to swarm.

    *Aquí*
The new sounds echo
a chamber older than memory.
Our *v*'s fling their arms open
and come back to us. *B*'s.
We have seen balas
faster than veins of light
etching the night sky.

They fill our heads with ringing.


## Medicine

*(after a print by Jeff Abbey Maldonado)*

Lacandona, the rain forest,
is a woman draped in solitude,

her hair a translucent cocoon.
In her lungs, a clearing

where stone pillars
hold arches of sky.

As tangled roots and loneliness
fill her tilted womb,

she turns her back on waiting.
Her dark shoulder passes

through temple walls
to the internal refuge

where she shapes masks
of creatures she imagines

spawning from her,
hatching from the splintered

shells of eggs
too thin to incubate.

There is a man under the tent
of her eyebrow,

an old ghost
in the slit of her stare.

There is a rustling
beneath her skin.

Axolotl, the lizard, slips
like green corn into her mouth,

clicks his toenails
against her teeth,

nestles in the harvest
under her tongue,

twists down
the stalk of her spine.

She searches for his tails
lost in her limbs,

caught on the branches of her ribs,
medicine to clear

the red clouds from her eyes,
draw the poison

from her punctured flesh
before it swims

into the seventh generation.
Sometimes, dusk soothes

her slashed back, cools its burns,
peels away the day's pain.

And if we turn
in the evening mist,

we can hear her
whisper our names.

## Our Language

When I sigh
I am breathing you
back out of me.
Like smoke you pause,
then melt into air.
You are often this intangible,
the silent *e* of love
or *hache* of hábito.

Háblame, you say,
yet my next breath
draws you in with the air
hissing past teeth
because I do not know
where I want you
or what awkward syntax
I'll leave twisted
in the whispering sheets.

The hush of your hands
reaches me from every shadow.
You kiss the slats of skin open
to the striped dawn
of the window blind.
You kiss these warm *l*'s
of light and depart.

In the caesura between hours and days,
weeks, I stroke watercolors.
The blue sinks deep
as the resonant pitch
of your vocal chords,
an anaphora of waves
lapping to the shore
until the paper is satiated.
I am not.

We work in English,
make love in Spanish,
and code-switch past our indecision.
On days filled with your absence,
I think in sinalefas
and trace you in the ring left
by my morning coffee cup.
If only I could touch
the amber circles of your eyes,
kiss your liquid pupils
when they dilate, enticed.
Then I'd be inside of you
as you so easily
fall into me.

I'd feel the constriction
of an *x* we cannot name,
the multilingual moan of *o*'s,
tense Spanish vowels
awaiting release.
Then the loose
twirling of an *erre*
down our spines,
down the soft sides of our arms,
líquidas vibrantes
of our blood.
This is how I want you—
at once within
and without

like a breath,
a sigh,
a language.


## Song

You shout my name
from beyond my dreams,
beyond the picture window
of this Rosarito beach house.
Rushing from bed to shore
I glimpse their backs—
volcanoes rising out of the sea.
Your back, a blue-black silhouette,
feet wet with the wash of morning waves.
Fountains spring from mammal minds,
my hands lifting a splash of sand.
I'm on my knees,
toes finding a cool prayer
beneath them, fingers pressing
sea foam to my temples,
while you open arms wide as a generation,
raise them to a compass point,
dive.
If you could reach them,
you would ride their fins
under the horizon,
then surf the crash of waves
left in their wake.
And if I could grasp
my own fear,
I'd drown it,
leave it breathless and blue
as this ocean,
as the brilliant backs
of whales
surfacing
for air.

Albino Carrillo

## De las Mujeres Tristes

My mother, beauty queen from Rincon, seemed
alone in her sadness. By this she meant
to show us how the world had given up
on her, how the angels made her bite
her lips like plums over and over
again. This much was true. She never knew
the words to fill her body with love, fearful
was she, reversed, who couldn't speak without

seeming terribly alone. You see
we saw the terrible place from where
this sadness grew. A mobile home, a point
on the map, all of her children angry,
fighting for something better: the green fields,
the beaming moon, and stars under Our Lady's feet.

## Animal Time

I cut loose the last rope, my way back home
when we were all lambs and we were all born.
Between the animal meat and my brain
I let go in sunlight: there was a father
in all of this, speaking a dull language
with his dry tongue until the sun goes out,
blue smoke filling the animals again.
I'll admit I don't know him, his back,

or his fine neck curving toward heaven—
in the evening when the thick trees turn black
and I am left to my body, slowly
the night rushes my mind to flame
and I cannot count the shuffling stars,
the holy holies who guard wicked doors.

## La Invención del Televisor Según Huitzilopochtli

He'll kill you if you whisper to the priest.
But in the garden behind the altar
he sits, the blue flickering of his dream
like the firefly he's crushing between
two fat fingers. For hours now he's painted
his lover's face with its electric juice:
because of the war that starves their children
they're awake and with their boredom take

the last pleasure from their bodies home
like something stolen or alone. It's here
he invents the first set, a radio,
later that first beautiful machine tuned
impossibly to all our frequencies,
to each heart on the continent, a gift.

## H. Writes His Dead Amigos for the Sake of Clarity

I will be with you again—our dogs running
in the piñon hills outside of Gallup, New Mexico, until sunset.
Nightly then, fat lamb steaks
or mutton stew and warm tortillas, the snow
march to the hot springs where bared to the stars
we'll talk all night of Proust or Hesse, we'll trade
sly homoerotic looks under the moon,
who, in washing our backs in light absolves us of any wrong.

Primarily, my lords,
the poems in the lost manuscript contained
a suppressed history of Dinetah as felt through the heart
of Dear Brother Begay, lost to us in alcoholic fire.
It was the witch of the south who in her bitterness took
flight with these words, these typed pages hacked out

one drunken morning in Albuquerque, to save
in a wooden box made from saw-ruined hands.

I will begin with you, amigos, whom I left on the roadside
long ago, walking away into the green, flowering hills
to live my life of hallways, children, and smoke—
where I live the northern sky hides everything
from me, near-sighted astronomer cosmonaut
who now must wander the boreal wilderness instead!
O, I still let my one dog roam the woods for any hint
of your kingdom—the black crows gathering,

the amethyst sky in January dusk.
Every tired moment I walk in the gray winter woods
my lords, it is for your presence that I long—while no
two men can be friends if they love the same woman, I pray
in the spirit world that our hounds and terriers
will cross that long bridge to find us
like warriors advancing on the dead hills to Mixtlán—holding hands,
singing savage songs to give us hope as we face the south wind.

## Lament for the chilero from Las Cruces

When the last twenty-pound gunnysacks
were carried to the car, the trunk
sagging, one brake light popped out in the rush
and struggle to get the filled sacks in,
the only thing he thought was that
going back was a sin: outside,
his brother was waiting for him,
dying. The chatter of the battered
Dodge running in the first cold
September morning was unlike
the sight of red-winged blackbirds
bursting from hedgerows and shorter

mesquite bushes lining the acequias—on
he swallowed briefly and was
in another world where the lit end
of his cigarette didn't signal death.

Great sacks of Big-Jim and Lumbre
he carried along at highway speeds somewhere
south of Taos, this Las Cruces boy
a chilero up north where they spoke
Spanish on the Colorado border
and into Alamosa county—
the locals didn't want the hot stuff.
So by the tracks where the Rio Grande & Western Railway
met the Santa Fe Line going east, he'd sit
in his champagne '72 Charger, lights on,
waiting for a train to take the rest
of his chile to Amarillo, or maybe even Austin.
Engineers he knew would stop their slow
loads to take a look at his "catch."
By the time he got back to Cruces
the waistband of his jeans were loose,

his pockets full of cash would feed
his sisters for a while. You see,
when his brother was a deputy they'd make
enough money for the whole farm and family
to go on. Their father, badly made
but unafraid of failure sat
in the house watching Lawrence Welk:
Parkinson's now kept him from his fields
and saw-horses, the outer
buildings on their land falling
into disrepair, chain-linked to keep
strays out. All the orchards around them
silent, shallow gray trees that once bore
pecans. For his gift of talk the world
rewarded him with this: a few acres
in a desert oasis where father couldn't even walk.

On those parcels grew the plants
that gave his little brood life and fire.
He often thought about chile, how
in the alkali fields his father had
abandoned for disease, these plants
thrived in full sun, reminding him
of how he'd cut into clay with sharp
steel tines designed to straighten
the land for horticulture.
The chilero's days started early.
Every spring, in April, he'd unpack
the seeds he'd kept in glass mason jars.
After seeding and months of coaxing the sky
for any bit of rain, after digging
two hundred feet down to an old aquifer,
the little white flowers would turn
and green flesh would thicken
at night, under a luminous black
triumph of stars and planets.

So in late August his brother
took a break from his life of domestic
disputes, gunshots, and muscle-bound
anger subdued by the force of his true
weapon: the cross on a chain around
his thick Mexican neck, a sterling silver
chain worn under his officer's black tie.
Not for pity's sake he'd arrest and jail
the most violent offenders, men down
with hate from the war who'd returned
to beat their wives, their children, anyone
who came looking. In the hot desert
air of Doña Ana country, then
the two brothers, after smoking
hand-rolled cigarettes and drinking
a pot of Café Combate, set out to the nearest

field to see the harvest. Back then,
small, brown mojados would stoop to cut
the chiles, and before Teófilo Flores bought
the first machines in 1973,
the whole valley picked by hand.
In the deaf fields of green chile
rolling like acres of green ribbon
along the Southern Pacific tracks
husky men, small men, caged men
by their own admission hefted sack
after sack onto the beds of pickup trucks,
the thick earth-meat of each pepper
seizing hunger, giving pig farmers
something to hope for. Because outside
their little county on the banks
of Rio Bravo lingered a single

sign of somewhat divine origin.
Blessed by its suddenness there
shone some nights beside a forest
of pecan trees and the hedgerows
of hard-packed earth a silver cross
fastened to a lamppost. Covered some
summers in the yellow pollen of Russian thistle
it still shone to guide the wetbacks
to the deeper part of life, so that their
sacrifices would be known under heaven.
Under that tall, tarred birch pole
Flores preached on Sundays about
the only true God and fed his children
corn tortillas at communion.
It was there, one morning, in the pulpit
that the vision first appeared—
as if he was scattering dry corn for his chickens and roosters,
he told his flock that the cross now shone
in unknown colors, pura, más pura
que las hermanas que viven en su casa.
And from the surrounding fields
the chiles grew, the workers slew
the impulse to rise up futilely

against each other or their God:
owning the field, and as His
sign a desert that grew each ranchita
enough chile to feed the family for winter.

But still on those parcels that grew
for life and fire the men stirred
uneasily in the toil, the women
drifted after years away
from anything real except the metate,
the hot stove, and the thick
tortillas kept warm under a cotton towel.
One afternoon at the end of July
it all came down to the strange cough
no one expected that summer—
of my whole life I'll tell you now—
no one expected the sickness
even when we sat up late
telling stories about the darkness,
what each of us had encountered
out there on the salt flats, at night.
In summer, you could hear
the fruit bats and the small green wrens
along the acequia, and the frogs calling
to the pale, sick moon, sick from the heat
and the drifting smoke in the sky.

When his brother first started to die,
I mean when he could count the days
some doctor in El Paso had given him,
he began to mount small crosses
cut from the Flores Farm's trees,
and hung, brightly, under the famous
cross Teófilo had blessed one summer
long ago when the ripe fields had finally
yielded their fruit in a tough, dry year.
There was no hope but to imagine
the same tough God who'd let them live
into one more season
would let him see winter. But lost
from the Cross he decided faithfully

to see his way through his present
life, no disaster ahead except in reason,
the end of days reining in,
the sky unfolding as he slept.
Left in the frost, left in the fact
of dull surprise and away from
the Savior, he could only savor
his last full year as one would
by driving all the way from Rincon
up to Alamosa with a truckload of chile,
fresh cut green from the holy fields.
When his brother first decided to see,
he was eating beans and warm flour tortillas
with Flores out in a mobile home
set up against the howling highway,
between two channels of the Rio Grande.
In that alkali moment he saw lights
sparking off the old man's head
and knew he had taken to flight—
the whole room glowed with consent,
impossible but there,
a wavering in each syllable, a throaty
thin white acceptance of the truth.
Aware now that he was going to die
all he wanted was that last cigarette,
black bullet for his lungs. You see,
wrung out of space he twisted his face
not quite in hate, but in a dull resolve
to go before the harvest ended, to drive
up north until his old car sputtered
at 10,000 feet somewhere in the Santa Fe
National Forest. Away up there in the cold,
dry air which would soothe his chest for good,
soothe any desert pains from the past
that kept him clutching his hard-working
heart. That hard muscle desperate
to keep beating, that hard muscle desperate
to keep the car in gear to climb the highest hills,
the small forest towns with the best markets ever.

Steven Cordova

## Testing Positive

The universe at times is simply that which lies
above—often a naked lightbulb disturbs.
Larvae make their earth in a chest of blond-
wood drawers; winter breaks; and a sweater
slips over me—fabric thin with holes.
Above me, men's eyes have starred open,
collapsed to seism. The universe when they fell
off me became cliché, became cracked ceiling.

Why fear my rise to the water-stain peel of death?
Today I watched an old man in a barber's chair.
His universe was the woman who, mortician-like,
clipped, circled, her legs scissoring air,
her breath and comb caterpillars on his face
and how she trimmed his eyebrows with great care.

## Sissy Boy

When they first came, panting, begging
at back doors, grandparents laid out
scraps of food. Grandchildren stroked
a thin flank, a small trembling spine.
And they remained and multiplied.

They took to running in packs that barked
and turned the whole block in its sleep.

One boy dreams hunger, poison
hissing. He rolls off the bed.
A breath escapes in a rush across linoleum.

His own mother made the call.
Whining, baying, they struggled,
but they were nothing more than strays,

a haze of bristle and fur,
to be netted, caged.

Now streets lay quiet, no howling
or mating. Trampled gardens unfurl.
Trash cans brim their empties.
And *mamasitas*—they sigh,
content without the sound of a wanton dog
defending itself in the middle of night,
fending off the fickle pack that turns on it,
the whimpering of the weak-haunched.

## Across a Table

"I'm glad you're positive."
"I'm glad you're positive,

too, though, of course, I wish
you weren't." I wish you weren't

either is the response I expect,
and you say nothing.

And who can blame you?
Not me. I'm not the one

who'll call you after dinner and a movie.
You're not the one who'll call me.

We both know we have
that—what?—that ultimate date

one night to come, one bright morning.
Who can blame us? Not the forks

and not the knives that carry on
and do the heavy lifting now.

# Meditations on the Jordaan

How you stirred & said, "Hold me," & holding you I imagined it was
    me pulling you through your tunnel of that day's dreams.

How I assured you, "I wrote down those lines, before I forgot." How,
    mouth full of sleep, you answered, "Poor little birds, trapped in
    paper cages."

How you looked up & said, "Tell me again how long you're here," & it
    had nothing to do with T-cells or hospital beds. Everything with
    our bed.

How you tried to teach me the long *o*, the short *e* of your name. How
    they were too short, too long, too little a time on my tongue.

How every morning the peal of bicycle bells, the sigh of the tram. The
    sound & shadow of a bird's wings flapping the morning we
    fought.

How you pedaled me past the Eerste Looiersdwarsstraat, right & east
    past three, four canals, left at the Singel.

How two days before departure there were three petals scattered
    about, two wilted flowers in the vase. One in full bloom.


# Daydream to You

*To be read aloud in a woman's voice with a Russian accent*

Of him much is written; little of Me—Me,
the Daydream.
       Mr. Dream, ha! He must live
with the brouhaha of the psychobabble paparazzi while
I am free to walk to the streets with less . . . pizzazz.
Does your therapist ask you please
to write down your daydreams?

No, he does not.
        No matter. I am there
when you shake the handsome stranger's hand,
when you cut open the patient's gut . . .

Little of what I put into your head comes true.
But what do you want? I am a full-bodied,
voluptuous woman, but I can work only
with what I have to work. I guess that
I—Daydream—I am like life. I am
a bitch. But I feel very close to you
in your "disappointments." You can forgive

me if all this is confusing, bizarre?
It is how I work, my charm.
Oh, please to offer me a cigarette?

[You light the match. Ms. Daydream leans in, then exhales.]

Rebuke me, my darling, and you rebuke yourself—
that much I have in common with big-shot Mr. Dream.

## In Your Defense

A TV jingle makes its tinny way into your recurring dream, proof that
dreams are not so strong as some would have it. A mere "no" falling
from a set of lips, a rejection in the form of a form letter, have forced
many a dream to wake and smell the coffee. And do you see? Already
you've confused night with daydream, fantasy with exaggeration. This,
in your defense, is a common error. He said, "What a nightmare!" And
he didn't mean that he'd just returned from sleep. He meant that on his
way to you he stood and was jostled on a crowded underground car.

If it sounds as though you're down on dreams—or him—you aren't
and you are. With dreams we can be in two places. Your cat naps. She
is in your bed meowing a muted meow—some dream-version of you,

maybe, snatches her latest precious plaything away. She twitches but can't shake herself to consciousness—some dream-bird she wants to kill escapes. (Easier—isn't it?—to say cat when you meant once he was in your bed—and spoke to another in his sleep. To say kill, when you meant love.)

A good day can be dream-like. You think, "I'll wake and ruin this." But you don't wake. You fall to sleep. Later—months, years, it won't matter because it will seem a lifetime—you'll wake. A cold room, just you, the cat. The music will play like an insult, yesterday's soundtrack. You'll throw back the sheets, wipe your mouth, switch it off.

## Pecking Orders

Here one rooster and two hens
leave a trail in sand some truant
wind will lift. My eyes, once
green and globed as a grape,
fade to hazel, flatten to gray:

plucking a handful of fruit,
what a cool relief that was
in the wavering air of this small town.
Sand dripped from my scalp,
drizzled from the dry ford of my ear.

And when a grape seemed too young,
I stood on tiptoe and balanced it
high on a refrigerator shelf,
sure that father's twin sisters
would eat it. They always did.

His sisters, they said father
was handsome, that he never
drank his green eyes red,
never beat his wife. They said
he pushed her around, but just a little,

the way their father did their mother,
a little. High noon again, and again
I rise, waiting for the cloud
who would lift me
in her dark and purpled arms.

## Of Sorts

You're faithful to that morning diary entry—that date, of sorts, with yourself—to start-time 9:00 A.M., the appointment with the doctor's cold scope at noon. You say good-bye and hello. You're faithful to each one, one by one. And in your dreams at night you're a bigger infidel. To begin, you're in the home you've made for yourself; then, without so much as a kiss to all you've made, without the wink but the rapid movement of an eye, you're in a home others made for you. And though you're not a child anymore, everything is as it was when you were five, or nine. Then, more movement, and you're in a place you've never been; a place you didn't plan to go; but a place you did buy the ticket to. With dreams—you're in luck—it's round trip. Awake again you must recount out loud this dream that philanders between present, past, and future. Or write it down. Or it will leave you. You're awake again, and must attend to something all too real, the need to pee, to expel what, for such a short time, was yours and yours alone.

## At the Delacourt

    Two swans:  the swan
on the lake  and the swan reflected
    on the surface of . . .  Shall we call it Swan Lake?

Two theaters:  theater on Swan Lake
    and, on its shore,  an outdoor theater
host this evening  to a play in media res.

All this doubling!  It has me believing
    I can see one actor  standing on the stage
and the same actor  reflected on its surface,

    the actor's "real"  character standing,
fictional character  reflected.
    I'm not sure  what I'm saying

except that since yesterday  I've been unable to move
    the left side of my face—  it's nothing,
a mild case  of Bell's Palsy,

not HIV-related.  My penchant for the frown and scowl
    will live again.  Ignorant for now
and at the Delacourt  I'm doubled too:

    I sit calmly  watching *Measure*
*for Measure;* I tremble  inside myself as
    the reflection of the swan  on Swan Lake must tremble

in the wings.  I bargain with God.
    And I refuse  to compromise.
*If You make me all  right, I swear I'll never . . .*

    *Oh, to hell  with You.*
Bored, the swans  fly east
    until, that is, the swan  above the water, in the air,

flaps past the border  of Swan Lake,
    and the reflected swan's no more.
No. Now there's just the one.

# Driving toward Lake Superior

A fire burned here.
Black—lifeless?—a stand of trees
    holds its position,

a ghost regiment
    demanding reparation.
Let memory stand:

We start the car, move
    on. It's not an empty threat—
their stand to our stand.


              *


Under bluest sky,
    three men drive toward a blue
sky, sky all around.

*You can't run, you know,*
*not from God.* This must be what
    that means, this deep blue

dome. Though clouds gather
    now. And now it rains. Heaven
cools its flame-blue burn.

Eduardo C. Corral

## Night Gives to Things the Turning Beauty of Leaves

The distant lights
    of Tucson
scattered like salt
    along the horizon.
Indigo-peaked
    mountains. A pack

of wild dogs
    chase quail.
Their barks lacquer
    the tail feathers
of the quail. The dogs
    pause, raise

their dark snouts . . .
    Beneath the arms of
a saguaro my parents
    make love.
Father's chest gleams.
    Mother tilts

her chin up, takes in
    her mouth
the gold crucifix
    roped around
his throat. The stars
    above them

and the sperm
    inside her swimming
frantically toward
    the moon.

## Ditat Deus

**1**

In high school I worked as a bag boy. To prevent shoplifting my boss had me follow the Mexicans and the Native Americans around the grocery store. I was slightly troubled by this. So I only followed the handsome men.

**2**

I learned how to make love to a man
by touching my father.

I would unlace his work boots,
pull off his socks,

& drag my thumbs
along the arches of his feet.

When he slept I would trace
the veins of his neck,

blue beneath my fingertip.
He would lift me each morning

onto the bathroom counter,
dot my small palms

with dollops of shaving cream
so I could lather his face.

## There Is a Light that Never Goes Out

Red leaves crackling
beneath our bare feet,
mother & I follow
a peacock through an orchard,
black markings etched on its narrow back

like the claw prints
of swallows in mud. Mother's floral dress
    troubled by a breeze—
            as the dress billows,
        the larkspur buds blossom,
release their scent, crushed fennel seeds . . .
    A twig snaps.
The peacock unfurls its enormous tail
    against a stack of fruit crates,
            & once again
    I'm a boy of eight peering
through his mother's bedroom window:
        an oval mirror,
    like a peacock feather, echoes
            her powdered eyes
                as she sits naked,
combing her long hair in the minutes
            before dusk
    when the dullest objects,
say a hairbrush, gather enough light to shine.

## Pear

Middle child, conqueror
of tree houses, my brother bites a pear,
the bite mark casts a pale light

that illuminates the storybook on his desk.
His favorite illustration: children
playing tug-of-war

beneath the sprawling branches of an oak.
Boys versus girls. He runs
his thumb over the face

of the tallest girl. Her socks
embroidered with yellow rosettes.
He bites the pear again, the light increases,

enough for him to notice,
for the first time, the silver cross
around the girl's neck.

If mother reads to him from the book,
he begs her to pronounce
the name of the girl. She insists

her name isn't embedded in the story.
So he's taken the jangling
of mother's copper bangles as she turns

the pages for her name.
He adores the girl's intense grip
on the rope. He can't read. Not yet.

He glances at his hands,
and though holding a pear,
feels rope sliding between his palms.


## To a Mojado Who Died Crossing the Desert

After a storm, saguaros glisten
                      like mint trombones.
        Sometimes a coyote leaps
over creosote.
               Hush.
The sand calls out for more footprints.
                  A crack in a boulder
can never be an entrance
                     to a cathedral,
but a mouse can be torn open

like an orange.

Hush.

The arroyo is the color of rust.

Sometimes a gust of snow

floats across the water

as gracefully as a bride.

## Monologue of a Vulture's Shadow

I long to return to my master

who knew neither fear nor patience.

My master who years ago spiraled

above a woman

trudging through the desert.

She raised her face & cursed us:

*Black Torches of Plague, Turd Blossoms.*

She lashed out with her hands,

pinned me to her shoulders.

I went slack.

I called for my master.

I fell across her shoulders like a black shawl.

Now I'm kept on the shelf of an armoire:

perfumed,

my edges embroidered with red thread.

She anchors me to her dress with a cameo of a bird

clutching prey,

as if to remind me of when my master flew close to the desert floor

& I darkened the arroyos

& the jade geometry of fallen saguaros.

How could I forget?

Often my master soared so high

I ceased to blacken the earth.

What became of me in those moments?

But the scent of decay always lured my master

earthward.

As my master ate, I ate.

## Midnight Coffee: Rafael Rodriguez Rapún, 1936

O my arrow-eyed lover, sugar, radiant &
      scattered around my heels,
brings back the evening when the first shafts of moonlight
         piercing a tall bedroom window
were crumbled in your palms, then sprinkled across the floor like
      snow
        whose brilliance amplified
as I extinguished the candles of the candelabra—
      Lorca, an olive-scented breeze rustling the leaves
of the lilac-stenciled wallpaper cooled the lengthening trail of sudor
         rolling down my torso.
Our bodies lit by the glare rising from the snow.
        Your guitar on a chair, scoured by moonlight,
a striped moon stamped in its interior . . .
      Your presence still seduces my eye: magnolia blossoms withering
        on a sill, the cuffs they tore from your sleeves.
A silver kettle sings, steam rising, dissipating—
        Andalusian ghost undressing.

## Julio Galan: *Misael*: Oil, Acrylic, Mixed Media on Canvas: 2001

again and again he shuffled a deck of cards/ a small accordion

in his hands/ to be a man/ to be a tree/ or even something less/ a
    plank

the wounds along his shoulder/ salmon leaping out of black water

# Poem after Frida Kahlo's Painting
## *The Broken Column*

### 1

On a bench, beneath a candle-lit window
whose sheer curtains resemble honey
sliding down a jar, Kahlo lifts her skirts.

A brown monkey chews a tobacco leaf
between her calves, tail brushing her thigh.
A skirt falls, its hem splashes on the concrete

like urine. A ruby ring on her forefinger.
No, the tip of her cigarette. Smoke rising.
The long hair of an old woman drowning.

### 2

Once a man offered me his heart like a glass of water. No, once . . .
Here's a joke for you. Why do Mexicans make tamales at Christmas?
So they have something to unwrap. A lover told me that. I stared into
his eyes believing the brown surrounding his pupils were rings, like
Saturn's. I have to sit down to say this. Once a man offered me his
heart, and I said no. Not because I didn't love him. Not because he was
a beast or white—I couldn't love him. Do you understand? In bed while
we slept, our bodies inches apart, the dark between our flesh a wick. It
was burning down. And he couldn't feel it.

### 3

Ask me anything.

### 4

I want to find the perfect shade of red. Say that.

### 5

A shadow drapes itself on an apple branch. Slow. Slowly. Jade moss
on the trunk intensifies like applause. Wind-braid wrapped around my
neck, unraveling: cold hair cascading toward my shoulders—July 23,
1997.

**6**

*Ladies and Gentlemen once again I would like to begin with the wound.*
*—Joseph Beuys*

**7**

An oval basket of roses on a dresser,
petals across the carpet, candle flames blown off their wicks.
Diego sleeps! Blue sheets pulled to his waist.
A fly lands on his right eyelid,

and for a moment it looks like one eye is open.
Jumping onto the bed, a monkey begins to lick the sweat
pooling in the hollow of his chest. Under a nightstand lamp
a drawing of Stalin—the light silvering the metallic ink

of the uniform buttons.

**8**

Constellations of coins scatter copper and silver light onto the butcher
paper taped above a dresser.
Crystal pitcher full of milk, arranged with lilies.

Torn sketch on the floor.

Through the window, sky like a torn sketch of the ocean.

Kahlo glaring at a self-portrait
as if her gaze were responsible for holding it to the wall.

**9**

The perfect shade of red:
the stain on an arrow pulled out of a dove.

**10**

Under the cold scaffolding of winter my love took me for a walk
through the desert. My breath crumbling like bread.
Under the cold scaffolding of winter my love took me for a stroll
through the desert. My breath crumbling like bread.

Under the cold scaffolding of winter my love took me through the
desert. My breath crumbling like bread.

### 11

Kahlo undresses in front of a mirror.
Her spine, a pouring of sand
through an hourglass
of blood.
Her hands
clutching the linen
draping the lower half
of her body, her fingers lost in its pleats.

### 12

A mirror remembering water.

David Dominguez

# Pig

I pulled into Galdini Sausage at noon.
The workers walked out of production
and swatted away the flies desperate for pork.
Pork gripped the men and was everywhere,
in the form of blood, in the form of fat,
and in pink meat stuck to the workers' shoes.
Outside, eighty-pound boxes of pork
melted under the sun, and as the sun worked,
the blood and fat grew soft, and the boxes,
lined with wax, became like thin paper soaked in oil.
Mack trucks came in with unprocessed pork
and took out chorizo, linguica, hot links, and sausage:
German, Sweet, Breakfast, Hot, and Mild.
One man stood straight up into the sky,
closed his eyes, and with his thumb and forefinger,
worked out bits of meat from his eyelashes
glistening like black grease under the sun.
The air conditioner in Mr. Galdini's office
made the papers from his desk float onto the floor.
He gave me a hard hat, a smock, an apron, and a hairnet.
"You're in there," he said and lifted the blinds
of a window that partitioned his office from production.
He stood, gut pushed out, and his whole body
swayed with ease as we watched the workers walk out,
humpbacked under the unyielding memory of pig.


# Fingers

Because of the frozen meat and a silver ring,
my index finger swelled and dimmed.
The men held down my wrist and used a saw.
I fought back the need to squirm and watched
where the nicked-up teeth missed

and the scars began to form.
I remember the day Julio longed to go home.
Nothing passed time like work,
unconscious work when the bones pounded
and the muscles stretched.
So when the stuffer jammed, Julio jumped on a stool,
lowered half his body into the machine,
and when his thigh brushed against the go button,
the blade moved an inch
and sliced off his index finger.
I wiped the blood and thought about Julio,
how he did not cry out,
how he asked for my smock
and held his hand against his chest,
how he pushed away those who tried to help.
How the finger was never found.
But most of all, I thought about myself:
would I have screamed, could I have taken the pain,
walked outside to the employee pay phone,
and, with good hand still held steady, dialed 9-1-1?

## Mexicali

See it in the monsoon winds
   that wrestle the night in the vacant lots.

In the *masa* slapped over the iron stoves
   where the women and the *chisme* are always happy.

In the eye of a dead crow crying out,
   "All life is delicate, all life is delicate."

At night, the wall disappears,
   and the lights on top look like stars.

A man finds it in his chest and drums,
        *Boombababoombababoom*, and his woman

sways her hips, "*Ándale*," she says, "*ándale mi amor*."
        Make it yours, lean into the ocotillo,

and beyond the spikes and the petals of fire,
        below the surface of the desert and the black roots,

hold out your tongue and wait
        for the arched tail of the scorpion.


## Empty Lot

My wife and I stand alone at the curb and stare
at the black numbers that mark our address.
We long for lumber, concrete,
copper tubing, stucco, and glass.
Empty fast-food cartons
tumble across the lot,
a crow pecks at the innards of a paper sack,
caws, dunks its head, and flies off,
a French fry in its beak,
this dirt the bird's home more than mine.
Twenty-five feet from the road,
my heel frames the front door, the entryway,
and dots a path toward
the kitchen and the gable window
where the sunlight will nestle on the sill,
on the backs of the dogs,
and in the cats' narrow eyes.
I want our house built:
a place for my wife to sit and read magazines,
to sip coffee at the table—
the books stacked, the door open,

ratcheting sprinkler head and water
the only sounds we hear.
Across the street, at four o'clock,
the construction workers open an ice chest
and sip beer in a truck.
*Rancheras* bounce on their radio.
I take my wife and dance.
My fingers cup the curve
that slides below her ribs,
and she squeezes my hands so that
it stays there where later
I'll rest my chin as we lay
along the creek listening to the current.
The men across the street
turn up the music and watch us dance.
This is the only floor we own,
a floor covered with dirt clods, weeds, and the ants
vanishing into the sacred
hallways of home.

## Framework

At the lot, we walk through the entryway,
a dizzying lattice of pine 2x4s.
The air smells of timber and sawdust,
and the rooms are filled with
fog dripping onto the slab.
My wife doesn't like the mango I bought her.
It's soft, unsymmetrical, and the pulp is splotchy.
A wayward dove has built
her nest in my new house.
She has lodged her life among
beams where the roof will sit.
The nest's brilliance is delicate:
weeds, insulation, and twine.
I lean, macho-like, against a 2x4,
but it gives where nails have split the wood.

I fall and brush off my palms.
My wife wants tile, and we can't afford it.
I'd like to do one thing right:
I want to be the kind of man who changes
his oil and brakes in the driveway,
a man, toolbox at his side, who can sort through
junkyards and find an alternator,
a man who knows plumbing, electricity, and concrete.
Instead, skinny men from Mexico,
with fire and muscle in their forearms and fists,
maintain my cars and build my house.
I turn sharply and announce,
"I'll install the tile myself, 1,000 square feet."
My wife's eyes roll, and she points:
I've torn my shirt on a nail.

# Roof

At lunch, I go watch the Mexicanos
who are putting the ceiling on my house.
They don't like me the moment
I park at the curb.
Extension cords crisscross the slab.
I nod at the fellow with the saw.
He's watching my feet,
nervous I'll trip and pull
the diamond-cut teeth
through skin, veins, and bones.
They have names for me: *pocho*, *gringo*.
The one with the nail gun nods
but before I look away
he punches three-pennies into a board:
I can take a hint.
Days ago, I saw a nest in the beams.
Now it lies on the floor,
a dove's refuge smashed under a boot.

# Chicago Title

The rain is rising along the avenues
in downtown Selma, where my wife and I
are signing piles of paper thick as reams.
She is touching my wrist with her fingers
to stop me from going mad under the
office's fluttering fluorescent lights.
The print is impossibly tiny,
and I know I'll never read it all.
Still, I pretend to understand contracts,
raising my sweaty fist to my chin,
and squinting in a doubting way,
but all I need to see are "Terms."
What makes me madder is trying to get
how it works, how my signature ties
to my neck thirty years of debt,
how my name entitles me to the keys
that unlock the front door and lock out
the world rising and falling like water
along the busy sidewalks, so I give my
attention to a few other mysteries
as I sign away my life: how the rain
keeps me at an open window for hours,
how my wife still smells of her perfumes
even after she refuses to shower
and wastes the day under a blanket,
how all I need is hot chocolate and bread,
wine, grape leaves, and olives,
and how I enjoy snoring wet dogs at my feet.
Perhaps some mysteries are better left
unanswered: the joy of house keys sliding
across the table, or how my wife's fingers
touch my wrist on a rainy day in Selma.

# Cowboy

As I walk into the Verona Café, *I am profoundly happy.*
My work boots clunk with each step,
and at the cashier's counter, I order black coffee.
I can't help myself, so I inspect the floor's workmanship,
and at once I see how sloppily
each tile was installed along the bottom of the counter.
When I take my change, the employee sees
my hands are covered with scratches and dust
and says, "Thank you, Sir."
In the café's brightest corner,
an old man lowers his newspaper.
We exchange manly nods—
the workingman's code for, "Hello."
Today, I installed the last tiles in my new house,
tiles I had avoided because
they had to wrap around the doorframes,
tiles requiring templates and hours to cut,
but they, too, are done—
slapped with thinset and grout.
This afternoon, I love that I am wearing jeans,
that my T-shirt is gray,
that my leather work gloves are shoved into my back pocket,
and that the cold wind rushes against my face
as I merge onto Highway 99
and my Mustang roars.

# Elwood

This morning, from the window,
I watched our gardeners roll out
4,000 square feet of hybrid Bermuda,

green as a jelly bean and so soft
that I couldn't wait for it
to tickle my wife's feet.

I dabbed my face with a towel
and felt good, since there was
no blood dotting my face,

put on a wrinkle-free shirt,
grabbed my bag—lecture notes done,
the week's reading fresh in my head—

and sipped coffee while I waited
for the car to warm up,
windows open, radio blasting.

But twelve miles from home,
the temperature gauge shot up,
and the steering wheel locked.

Roadside, I popped the hood,
and at first, I thought a rat
was caught in the fan belt,

but slowly the outline
of a larger animal became
distinct against the grease.

I leaned over the engine block,
listened to its gasping,
and thought, "I killed a fox or a coyote."

One hind leg was mangled and burned,
and after I used the tire iron
to work it free, after

it slipped onto the pavement,
I knew it was my cat because
of the dark markings along his back.

He clawed at the pavement,
shocked over his shorn ear
and his eye that had popped out.

I thought about the way he chased
my wristwatch's reflection
on the wall when I ate dinner.

Tire iron locked in my fist,
I considered ending it there:
who knows what mocker he was stalking

when gardeners came or how he was feeling
when he saw tools drop from
their trucks and fill the yard,

who knows what he was fearing
when he jumped under my hood
to ditch the pandemonium of strangers,

who knows how his day was going
before I smiled at the morning
and started the car?

John Olivares Espinoza

# Aching Knees in Palm Springs

One gray Thursday in winter break,
Albert and I plucked patches of grass
From petunia beds wide as swimming pools
Within a condo complex; one-story stucco blocks
For old men who wipe sweat with dollar bills.
We spent our school vacations in shivers:
Raking, trimming, and mowing frosted yards with Dad.
At the eighth hour of kneeling,
The weight on my knees was too much for me.
For each fistful of grass, I stood up to stretch
And let the cold air sneak under my shirt.
When Dad noticed the weeds slowly filling the can,
He turned to me red-faced and said,
*You're packing down the dirt, kneel on the lawn*
*And weed the beds from there.* I said,
*I am at least entitled to some circulation . . .*
I kept the truth from slipping past my chapped lips,
How I didn't care about dirt and weeds
From a bourgeoisie's garden—these few men
I learned about in Sociology class—
Who raked in more hundred-dollar bills
Than I did citrus leaves in a day.
I wanted to tell Dad that these men didn't care
If Mexicans spent ten hours—or even a lifetime,
Weeding out the same bed the following week.
To only tell him about the hours I felt wasted,
When we could've rested our sore backs on a bed
And drowned in the lake of a much deserved sleep,
Or sailed through Tierra del Fuego, us standing
On the deck and never bowing, not even to the sun.
Or how he could have learned to read,
And I would finally show him a poem I wrote.
But I didn't. Because I knew what he would say—
*It's the only way to put you through school—this oily sweat.*
I kept my tongue hidden behind my teeth,
And watched my brother hunched over, tossing weeds
And years inside a green plastic can without a word.

# Contemporary American Hunger

We were the newest broke Mexicans to settle in Indio,
Mom having quit her job at school
To rest her neck, tense from hovering
Like a desk lamp over the Special-Ed kids.
Albert and I, barely hip-high
To our mother, unaware of our budget,
Salivated as we thought about the dry buns,
The Grade B patties of Argentine beef at McDonald's—
For what our TV eyes believed was the best lunch in town.

At McD's, we paid for two cheeseburgers.
Mom pulled out her blue purse, laid out
A buck thirty-eight—
Two dull quarters,
Six dimes, five nickels,
And three parking-lot pennies.
The cashier's forefinger counted
The change as Mom held up the line,
While the regulars tapped
Their feet behind her. She stood red-faced,
For these burgers slid towards her
On a bright plastic tray.

Bun by bun, Mom bulldozed
With a plastic knife the spread of ketchup,
Mustard and chopped onion
Before slicing the burgers to give each of her sons a half.
Satisfied, we ventured through a rainbow
Of tubes and balls with the other kids,
Their stomachs full of Big Macs or Happy Meals.
But we were happy too—better than staying
At home on a Saturday
Eating potato tacos after our yard chores.
Did Mom sit there and watch us play?
I only remember her fingers neatly wrapping
The remaining half in the greasy red and yellow paper,
Then tucking the lump away in her purse, sustenance for later.

# Learning Economics at Gemco

My mother pushes a grocery cart,
I tug at her blue, pleated skirt.

She puts her change into my hands,
For the old soul slumped against the wall,
His gray mouth covered by a beard of wind and dirt.

I place the coins into his cupped hands
And he stacks two neat columns of cents
Next to his seat on the curb.
He nods his chin, half-solemnly.

I turn back to mother,
Suddenly a cop—he came out of nowhere—
Tells me *Take the money back.*
I brush the coins
Back into my palms like table crumbs.
As the old man,
Silent as those pennies,
Gets cuffed and hauled off to jail.
I ask Mom why?—
We only tried to help.

The cop says bums make thirty bucks a week
Begging for change
And are not too unhappy
When arrested
Since they get food, shelter,
And a hot shower for at least a week.

My mother pushes the grocery cart without a word,
Knowing that as newlyweds she begged outside markets for change
While Dad stole bread and sliced honey-ham inside.

# Las Cucarachas

Roaches sniff
  with their two
    strands of hair
      around the kitchen
    and slip through
  the cereal box-tops
as easily as any envelope
  slides beneath a door.
    They munch on dry corn
     flakes you thought
    were raisin bran.
  In the bathroom,
 they dip their faces
in the uncapped
 toothpaste and massage
 their bellies
   against the bristles
    of your toothbrush.
  At night, they climb
  over the ravine
 of your mouth
while you snore
 and become the first
  things you see waking
   from a dream.
    They tickle your toes
   when you put on
  your boots.
When I turn on
the light before work
 I see them
  on their knees,
   elbows resting
  on the roach trap,
 pincers pressed
in prayer,

offering thanks
 and grace
  to a god who favors
   them with the lost
    harvest of the earth.

## The City of Date Fruits and Bullet Wounds

*for Alfred and Sam*

You're cruising the streets
        Of Indio, it's Friday,
        Late night in the city
Of date fruits and bullet wounds.
You're driving, your best friend
Next to you tugging
        At his seatbelt. Two more
        Are in the backseat:
The one sitting left stares at the neon
Lights of a 7-Eleven as you wait
For a left turn on Highway 111.
The other one sees two cars pull
        Up next to yours.
They've mistaken your best friend
For his older brother,
        Yell a few *fuck yous*
        And *watcha lookin' ats,*
Strike your car with beer bottles.
Each minute feels as long as a city
Block, not nearly as short as our lives.

                When you two were seven
                Or maybe ten, I remember
                You were skinny as my father's
                Yard rakes, and you were leaning
                Under a grapefruit tree.

Your plump best friend doing
Pull-ups on a branch,
My brother counting them off.
You grew up with your friend
Together like two grapefruits
On the same stem, the ones we
Peeled in the dusk
Of an October Monday.
What did you both not know
Of each other?
The first whiskers in the sink,
Fingers crawling under a skirt.
My brother always spoke
Of you two, side by side
In a world of mud-dark places
And dusty streets.
These memories spread thin
Like field dust on our shoes
After a short-cut home.
That's where we want
To go, right? But not the homes
Like our houses, but places like where
You bumped into my brother
And me outside the market,
When our grandfather was still breathing
Steadily. You were melting
Hershey Kisses between your teeth
And cheeks, your legs
Still broomsticks.
It's these places where we dropped
A little bit of our souls
Like loose pennies
From our pockets.

Alfred, stay like you are
    In my first memory:
Not when you're in your car and
    Two boys step out and fire.
    Not when you duck
Under the dashboard knowing glass

Can't stop a bullet any more
   Than a chest bone.
   *Fuck it*, you say, *I'm hit.*
   You throw yourself over
Your best friend like a blanket
Of flesh, take a few more
   Hits for his life,
Until some homeboys watching
From across the street
Scare off the locos with a few shots
Of their own. Your engine
Bleeds transmission oil.
   Your last breath cold
On your best friend's neck.
I only want the grapefruit
   Peels in the dirt,
   My brother and I
   In the parking lot
After a trip to the candy counter
With grandfather, unwrapping
One piece of chocolate after another.

## The Story My Grandfather Told My Mother
## a Few Months before His Death

Anoche, I fled this place of horrors. These viejos moaning for painkillers, they make me, they make me tire of them. I was fed up of its janitor's stink. To save the strength in my legs I slept for three days. The swelling in my feet deflated. The clock read half past twelve. I wore my paper gown without zapatos and walked along the highway's shoulder and stepped on every piedra. I stepped on bottle caps. I stepped on broken glass . . .

*And you didn't come across any coyotes out in the desert?*

I flung rocks at two or three. Bared my teeth and gums. Growled. Los coyotes weren't the problem though. The cars were. They drive faster en la noche, afraid of espíritus walking in the dark. I struggled against the car's air resistance, but lost my balance and tumbled on the shoulder with the Styrofoam cups. Before my body came to a stop, another car passed through and I rolled again. Then raced one more car after another, until I picked up wind and was somersaulting with the plastic bags. I hovered over an onion field and remembered I knew how to fly as a boy. Nightly, I flew over the fields to pick the next day's crops so there would be less work waiting. Below me, El Rancho Viejo, and I remembered how to land: one knee comes out, point the other leg down.

*Did you fly through the chimney?*

Why didn't I think about that? When I arrived at el rancho, I was too weak to unhook the chain and let myself in. And after all that trouble. I rested on a rock, doodled self-portraits in the dirt for every decade of my life, until I got my strength. I walked back to the nursing home and stepped on sticks of dried mesquite. I sneaked into bed without being missed. When I woke up you were here.

*Maybe it was a dream, Apá? It sounds like a dream.*

It was no sueño. Check beneath my feet for thorns. Check and pull them out.

# I Go Dreaming, Raking Leaves

It's been six years since I've strangled a rake,
Dragged its green teeth across grass,
And still I'm raking leaves during my sleep.
Citrus leaves abundant as body hair.
I rake a small pile, toss half into a plastic can
And another pile takes its place. The leaves never stop coming.
The same way one cleans a wound and the blood keeps rising.

# Network of Bone

### I

No muscle in sight. The sandwich flab
Circles across the navel like Saturn's rings.

Shoulders diving-board narrow.
Hips the width of a cereal box.

As the Greeks to their skies, someone
Once connects the constellation of Hercules
With the moles on my back.

### II

Though my arms appear thin enough to shatter midway a set of push-ups, my biceps are oranges covered in flesh. Darker skin from the elbow down, it's not a farmer's tan, but a gardener's—after summer months of mowing and raking in T-shirts from the previous school year, whose tears and holes have me looking back, holding on to nothing.

### III

I've seen men my age whose arms are bigger than my legs.

### IV

Even with the grace and speed of Mercury's wings
Donned on my ankles, these feet
Couldn't outrun an arthritic greyhound.

### V

I've learned patience through facial imperfections: cheeks scarred by scratching and the picking of high-school zits. My ears stick out like satellite dishes casting shadows of their own as I walk down a sidewalk at high noon. My nose—a question mark tracing back to Zapata, who opposed the state at every turn. Left eye out of focus because of slight astigmatism blurs the grace of the world, making the orange blossoms of La Quinta appear like desert snow. Teeth stained yellow with the constant sips of Coca-Cola, teeth straightened by metal brackets and wires, have now shifted out of place, like pebbles in Mojave wind. My hair, midnight waves receding from the shoreline.

**VI**

My heart beats endlessly behind
This visible network of bone.
My heart pumping evidently that this man
Walking the streets is not a skeleton out of coffin.

Gina Franco

# Everything Goes Down a Changeling

A great cloud of tiny insects—ingenious,
the summer light sifted through all those wings
like that, like a thought shifting
over a bog veined in bright water.
The air was coming down
with an imminent rain—I could feel it.
And you were there, shaking your head,
smiling at the camera though I felt slighted.
Everything goes down a changeling, you said.
You've got to have it how you can.
So it was hopeless already when I noticed
that my legs were running
with blood, with mosquitoes thickly drowning,
when you turned from me saying,
well, it's what you wanted.

# Darkling

It happened gradually. My hands, always behind me, sore
from picking at ropes, went first.
They began to feel light and hollow, though something prickled
beneath the skin. My fingers closed and fused,
my arms grew narrow and long
until they were twice the length of my body.
Then, my heart. It raced ahead of me
and tried to thrash its way out—
*philomel, philomel—*
I listened, afraid to speak.
I thought the hush could do me no harm.
But in silence my tongue was severed.
I'd watched it writhe on the ground in front of me, murmuring,
dividing, becoming forked before it slithered off.

When feathers finally appeared in patches, I saw
that you can live, mute and still, with a sharp desire
for your father's country, which is power.
Or you deny your name until it feels like strength,
and give away all but your scarlet hair,
for it might bring recognition
when you feel murderous, waiting, impatient to do nothing,
turning away from a spindly light that burns your eyes.
You sleep all day, wake fitfully in the evening,
dream of a lover as gentle as your father.
Out of any long-chosen habit you will be transformed
if you are living in want.
He will leave again, and he will return, of course he will.
He will leave, brandishing his coiled weapon
that makes you convulse with longing
to sing.

## Velvet

But inside her, there is always velvet,
velvet with its give and yield, the kind you
find at a pet store, a bin full of long
ears and noses busy snuffing up nerves
among the cedar chips and their eyes
opening wide as if rabbits couldn't know
what softness brings, as if they'd never know

the smell of something long stored away now
brought into light, and now, too, her mother
with a camera pointing at her, red
child on the lap of the Easter rabbit,
softness of the body hiding inside
the costume, eyes glinting from the wide holes
in the mask, not a single sobbing breath

of wind down the trail of mesquite and broom
foot-printing the hills of some rancher's land.
The bird dog lifts his ears to the sound
of velvet, the girl listens to the drawn
cries of a crow, her father walks
with the silence of the shotgun, waiting
for the pointer to find scent, the rabbit
at the end of it blinking, its wide eyes
shrinking from the scuffle of their feet like

velvet settling, laid over lines, drying
across the ceiling of an uncle's garage
where they talk inside the smell of salted
skin. At least three dollars for each good pelt
he says, and they scream like children when,
sleeves rolled over his forearms, he brings
the club down on their heads, saving
their feet for cheap key chains, for luck

that softness doesn't seem to have inside
of cages, chicken wire, tubes of water,
and sometimes boys who try kicking the cage
around to see what happens to velvet
tumbling. And, in the after quiet,
she bites the hands reaching toward her, so they
stone her, they open her belly and pull
some things out, open the pink albino
eye and groan at the fluid inside. Then they
bury the carcass without thinking first
of washing their sticky hands in the sink

before eating dinner, before setting
the table, in the still softness of her
beige room, she sits on the carpet picking
at the velveteen of Bunny's stuffed neck,
the rabbit's eyes dull with scratches, eyes left
behind on her bed at night when she stands
in the hall, hearing her father breathe in his room

in the darkness, on the futon, kicking
off the sheets. Awake from a fluid dream
of a woman's eyes staring from behind
a gag, her white skin settling in fat pools
around her, naked, bald. And a man's
voice said, *this is your rabbit*, so she woke
to this dream inside her, with his teeth wrapped
in her hair, and his hands inside her thighs
where he fingered her coldly. But it has
always been like this—wild, insidious,
and commanding because she gives to it,
fascinated by it and caught by it,
as velvet only listens and is quiet.

## These Years, in the Deepest Holes

A summer kite. My father's. It drifts high
over the cemetery gazing down on our little graves.
There is Linda who died in portions. Toes, calves,
thighs, amputated after a black widow bite.
There is Harold, still unmarked. My first suicide.
And someone else, the name escapes me, thrown
vehicle-free on the old intoxicating horseshoe turn.
Now panning back, a man's hand loosens the twine
a little, a little, and a girl picks through the bushes,
flushing cottontails with rocks and sticks,
and there, that is your voice—that is you
mocking epitaphs and plastic flowers. The train snagged
in mesquite, the father and daughter with their hands
at their sides. But where did you come from?
It's bad enough I see you everywhere else.
The man pulls weeds from a plot, his father's,
and tells the girl stories about giant catfish
who lurk these years in the deepest holes of the 'Frisco.

His face labors with words while he yanks,
his gloves stained with the habit of breaking clumps
from roots. You sit nearby and want me to watch you—
that is your way—but I am watching the girl,
listening to her listen. She is fishing
with her father. She remembers a river picnic,
the new bikini she wore, her father saying, come,
let's see how well it fits. Come on. Come here.
When she steps up close, he nods, approves.
She almost walks away but he pulls her
bottom down with a quick peek and laughs.
She toes the ground with past awkwardness,
and looks around for someplace to put it.
You stand behind her. Your arms are crossed,
for it is nothing, gazing down on the greater
scheme of things, most of the time, nothing.
She looks out at the flattened infant graves,
so many, they seem to multiply. They drift
under the earth, small bones. What becomes of them?
They lie in wait. They ascend in time. They return
to devour with their cries for attention.


## The Walk Like Old Habits

It seems unlikely, how the city repeats itself
without describing your life. Peeling billboards,
chinks in the walls. Girls on the corner make signs
to one another in the dust, balconies turn
from the beggars rearing up like mannequins
and you think truth is there, however unintelligible.
But it does not wake you to street names you imagine
said something adequate in the beginning, if ever
one street was not like the next, if ever this place
was not like Venice, not like Beijing, but itself
the first lone thing under the sun. Like the garden

before it was *their* garden: the sun before ritual,
before gods, sprouting from stones and fountains, mad, mad,
before all things unremarkable, as winter, as excrement.
Nor does the sudden maze of bicycles and storefronts
bring a word to mind, nothing more than concrete,
brick, glass, motion, all useless, really, though you
come across a woman who sorts through a box
of white fruit, her face pocked with scars
you might recognize should the moon appear full
to announce a point of origin or pleasure that is free
of mooning on every waterway you see. If only
love were free of spit and image, and image—interrupted
by the bells, bells, bells calling from towers
in churchyards where lie the beloved in crates—were
free of rivals. Laughter erupts from a place, many,
beyond the canals, the canals below chimneys
and cemeteries and temple steps, the steps
where old men watch boys mock them, now limping,
now drooling, now trying on an old man's palsy
leafing through a book: licks a deliberating finger,
turns to the pages like the living turn to bread.
The corpses. The guillotines reminiscent of lab rats
stand in for revolution in the square, the emperor
moves through the crowd like a crisis coming
to a head. Heads and more heads in the streets,
this street where you open your eyes and find, isn't it
strange, that you do not grieve the bare infant
you gather to yourself from the walk like old habits
reminding you that some things are new, this body
who wakes you, new hands, new eyes. So little
do you know yourself and the light you would make
even here, to the quick, embracing small things
that grasp you—it's me, it's me—that you
look up for the grounds of your blessings.

# The Earth Without

> I have known several who came back from there who now amuse
> themselves by talking of how it would be to go back and proceed to
> recover that which is lost, while others enjoy trying to find the reason
> why it was discovered at all.
> —The Journey of Coronado

To bed, I guess, that weary enough I can erase
for a night those accidents of spirit and flesh
who amuse themselves by bringing the lynch mob
behind me—whose old glittering eyes have made me
a guest in my mother's house, and an orphan,
and an illiterate, and a law-abiding whore. In whose eyes
I find my brother again, and dream him among the order
of fathers who negate me, just as I labored
to desert him in the desert, a rock pick in his belt, the shade
of his hat against miles of sand that dazzle the mind
with the tracks of those who followed, too, mulish,
towards veins of metal reaching through
the land up north, so rich, the mother lode, you can
dig it out with a spoon, so certain that bolas
de plata some four thousand pounds were found
even after the days Francisco Vasquez de Coronado
went seeking the cities of legend for God and gold.
That granted, the expedition of fourteen hundred men
and fifteen hundred animals did not find the riches
of which they had been told, that they arrived in this country
with swords and the pope when shovels and prayer
have profited better on the wayside, as it goes,
lined with the sun-bleached bones of unfortunate men.
The earth did not devour them, much as they
compassed—what a thing to do—to eat of its dust
all their days. Going south and further
south, I saw the adits carved into the high
red cliffs. They mouth the gritty attending silence
of the Coronado trail. I did not understand.

Consider: salt of the earth, sulfur, rain, copper, air,
rolling down in drops, seeping into the mineshafts,
bubbling, hissing in the limestone, weeping tears
over tears, following slow, indiscernible, involuntary,
relentless, it trails from the walls, eats with abandon,
rains. It makes its way in the dark, its crystalline habits,
its taste metallic and sweet, its incomprehensible electric
blue, so blue the gamblers carry it for luck and the women
say it protects against el ojo, is a necessary evil,
this bluestone, Roman vitriol, blue copperas, chalcanthite,
copper sulfate, all the makings of a caustic beginning.
One thing is clear. Blue water means copper, a lot of it,
resting just below the iron-red soil you see driving down
Route 666 into town past Cole's Pizza and the schoolyard,
the dealership, Maud's, the courthouse where I carved
my name into the old soft brick, and the river whose
hundred-year floods would bring my father to hang
St. Christopher around his neck, to call his son,
my brother, by the name of one so surely cast out
even the nomadic children of the sun might be
lifted up and carried from one turn to another
in his hands, as the river turns water. Be patient,
my love, I am telling you: in the crossing the light

breaks you, hailing, dying in cries, praising you
among tongues like white wings darting on the surface,
and below, where moss pulls at your legs, entrails
of legions, who have sworn themselves over to those who guard
your will against your will, say yes, indefinitely, here you
are at last, but where you thought you could get to
is not for you to end. What did you think?
That the whole would unfold at once in a breath, in birth,
this child at home, cast out, whose task in this world
is to carry you in his chest, behind his ribs, you,
pouring in, out, of the two halves of his heart?

I kept you wandering through the mazes
of the underground mines, far below the roots of the shrubs,
where blue water seeps through the shafts and bluestone
gathers in the veins. Against my will and yours, I held
the considerable weight of you in my hands. I dig
you up, find you watering the small swelling lawn, unearth
you in front of the little green-shingled company house
weeding a trellis of pink roses by the door and the cactus
you planted in the flowerbeds. You rake, dig into rock
and clay, break clods of earth in your hands, plant
seeds you buy at the company store. You hum
through copper wires running through my house.
I would have walked the earth without the earth
you walked—I would not have looked back—backbone, stone,
what are they doing now but looking up
from their work towards the sky, Díos mío,
in the east and the north, just beyond
the next border?—had you not decreed my silence.

Wise up, güerita. Spanish wasn't allowed.
Forced at gunpoint into cattle boxes, deported
to New Mexico, left in the desert. Communists,
enemy aliens, obstructing production in a time
of war. We strike. We await contracts with hands
at our brothers' throats. Walk the earth if you will,
since you will not find shelter in your father's
company—this much I promise—for that mouth.

It is unfortunate. Perhaps you would like to negotiate
the terms of the impasse (who would notice it).
Bear in mind: we wish to state one conclusion
with all the emphasis at our command. Every day
this difference is prolonged constitutes a threat
to our general welfare. We realize the stakes
are high. We understand why you have found it
difficult to reach an agreement. It is the nation itself,
however, which here has most at stake. No loss can
compare with what the country between you suffers.

Backcountry, wading next to you in the green pools
of the river. We bake fish on hot stones beside our fire,
watch the cliffs for bighorn scaling the rock
above us. Downstream, where the fig grows wild
we make our way to the abandoned mineshaft,
our destination. The bats have taken over
and the stench of their droppings stops us even as
the cavernous heart, so old, so difficult, pauses, is
silenced, sleeps by us patiently, even as
we are silenced in my memory of us transfixed
in its eye. We've come all this way to our ruins: all
but in our having known them, vanished.

Venessa Maria Engel-Fuentes

## Cebolla

*Mi abuelita dice que cuando*
*la cebolla*
*te hace llorar, es porque es*
*macho. Cebolla hombre.*
The men bring
tears to the eyes, she says. And, from
what I understand,
from the way certain wrinkles
lie on her face when she is sad and
full of her Bolivia,
I do not doubt this.
But we are different women.
Onions to me are not the same thing.
Our shared names
do not fit the
same way in our mouths. *No importa*—we still know what
the other means.
I wonder:
how many onions
has my abuela chopped in her life? How many
paper shells peeled away to make the
fingers and palms so smooth.
She has no more fingerprints.   They've worked
themselves inside out and now
face her blood rather than the blade.
She is my mother tongue, where I come from.
I breathe deep enough to
touch the bottoms of my lungs
when I know she's been cooking.
Check her eyes to see if she's been crying
Tearstain on a napkin
Abuela's history
adds another shell to mine.

I am looking forward to the day when
my wrinkly hands can be so calm.

## Como Park, 1975

She will forget
about the balloon
tied around her wrist.
Saturday afternoon melts
An ice cream sandwich at the zoo and the
polar bear gone crazy swimming
One thousand small circles
in his tank.
Someone who cares for her
will take a photo.
She running into
her shadow
a stretch of pavement
ready to skin a knee.
String that hangs from her hand
like a cough.
Her white socks a pair of candy cigarettes
warm from sweat and sugar.

## Hermanita, Hermanota

She
would have been a good
little sister.
I think of her all skinny fingered
and rootless like me.
I like to think she is thinking
of me somewhere.
*Hermanita, hermanota.*
I am romancing the idea,
wanting more than a global sisterhood kinda thing.
I'm talking about genetics.

Biology. A shared curve here or there
to the fingerprints.
A secret language and
giggles underneath the sheets.
Would we have similar memories of our
mother's belly sleeping
in the backs of our heads?
She would have been my
tiny anchor. I her mixed-up ocean.
Us searching for home. Finding it in the
movements pigeons follow as they fly
by the church
in a circle.
Our skinny fingers
prying open the dried lips
of our history. Demanding re-entry.
Kissing warmth and blood back in.

I believe she is out there.
*Hermanita, escúchame.*
There are too many colors
wrapped around each other.
Too much mutt blood. So much that it
mixes even with the earth,
*con esta tierra callada*, like water.
It moves with ferocity
underneath the surface. It moves
because it has to.
To find home
kneel down.
Put your tiny ear to the ground.
Put your finger on your pulse.
These will match, the currents of our mutt
blood moving.
*Qué bonito.*
I will meet you there,
our home *sin fronteras*
will recognize you by the dirt on your knees.

# Unit 502

You think you are tired of apartment life
the thin walls, neighbors just inches away with you
decked out in undies and socks.
The fridge laughs at your predicament, can
read your mind, while the television blinks dusty thoughts:
       What can he do to pull you back in.
Despite high ceilings and exposed brick
walls, you're positive a patio, a mud room
would cure you of
this longing. All of a sudden
even the dogs
look weepy. Moans come and go
from the next door neighbor's bedroom wall, your
living room wall. You blush and close your eyes.
The elevator bored silly from the same-old
breaks down again.
You pace, careful not to disturb 402,
wish for a fenced backyard, thick poplar tree
to shush summer away.

A trip to the farmer's market helps.
String beans and heirloom tomatoes smile at you.
They know.

# Glass Grapes

Gramma Anna's kitchen is dark.
Thick bars of song not even the
earliest birds have a name for. She
gives me good morning     glossy hand
flat against my heart.
She pulls sleep apart, sets me out for breakfast
milk, bowl, spoon. Music in full swing now,
Anna plugs in the coffee pot

washes her face, tugs and smoothes
ironed hair into a knot.
I lose myself to the percolator's
blink and hiccup      daydreaming a sugared streak
clear into my elbow.

Grampa Harry, like a cornfield,
rocks back and forth. His chair smart in the middle of things.
Porch, stoop, kitchen, wife.
He is good to look at, doesn't know
I own the corners of his house.
Hands in the couch cushions, laundry
breathing heavy on the line.

Scotch and milk cry together in a glass,
a wet ring on Grampa's coffee table.
This his display case: ashtray and pipes,
ceramic group of hands in prayer
forming a church house, and a bunch of
glass grapes; each a wish      a cast-iron question about
my papa. *Might come by,* Gramma says.
*He heard you're here,*
*child.* Grampa knows
better than *might,*
hollers, *Come here girl! Give Grampa a hug.*
He knows
the contents of my pockets very well.

# Record-Keeping

Wilson Jones with a five-dollar bill, all
Debts squared
Checks the sandwich board. Today a
Bowl of chowder and weak tea.
He's thinking clear again
About deadlines and empty ashtrays, dotted lines,

Keys. An endless string of destinations and
Phone calls. He carries them high
On a platter. Thinks:
*She's the bee's knees*
From across the fence.
Line cooks eye him from across
Cracked blue plate specials, their
Chicken-fried steaks spooning
With the peas and carrots.
Donuts sweat on a cake stand, an extra fifty cents
Glazes Wilson's walk home.
There are crumbs to sweep, the post has come, he
Wedges honey-coated postcards into
Gaps in his bookshelves.
Wilson is keeping time
Sweet on the tongue after
So much grit.

## Funeral

Mercedes washed clothes
the day her mother died
A piece of breath
lost in the river
Knuckles a row of four red dots
ready to grieve.

Because
her husband said so
the black dress hung
A sad fire in her closet
and the clouds outside a
length of string come undone.

Certainly it was over the dishwater
Mercedes cried while blessings

were laid out    An empty chair
by all the wreaths of margaritas and lilies
Little white flowers to knit into a scarf
warm the soft line of neck.

Her prayer that afternoon a clothespin
in her hand
The church
full of sleepy eyes and ash
La Virgen keeping watch
over so many lit candles.

## Pinkie

Give me your pinkie
*mujer*
I promise you five snowflakes
each perfect
six sided
*bien* pretty kept in a box
I'm telling you,
The moment sparrows
all bone and bread
start their noise in the trees
               that Frida-blue hour the best time for prayer
I know the North Shore
in you
Lake water    Two rocks
An afghan caught between cushions
I know Colombia
in you
That pearl on your finger from
so far away.
Mother tongue wrapped tight in memory
Bit of white gold,
one dozen daffodils.

## Insomnia

The moon finds me and my house
a mess again.

I collect the moon from
patches of grass      from

between your teeth.
If I give you this pen
I'd trust you less.

You'd write secret passwords on
the backs of old maps
instead of writing

letters to me      my name stitched
neat along the margins.

While the neighbors vibrate and
chase the moon up a lamppost
this pen digs a hole

only your hands
know how to undo.

Kevin A. González

# The Night Tito Trinidad KO'ed Fernando Vargas

*San Juan, Puerto Rico*

I rode in the bed of a pickup truck,
raising a Corona to toast the moon.

Six of us, we dumped ice & a case
onto the rugged metal—no Styrofoam relief,

no white custom to keep us cool.
We didn't care the bottles rolled

into each other, their acute chime
beneath the blasting horns & gunshots

echoing off the curb's molded lip.
We didn't care, in the numb pool

of ice & glass, that we live in a colony
& the stripes of our waving flag

yield a black shadow under
pirated fireworks. We wanted only

the sour smiles of lemons wrung
into our bottles, our tanned skin

soothed by something cool, the touch
of fingers on a crisp steering wheel.

We wanted the unofficial midnight parade
to wind past the Dos Hermanos Bridge

& Puerta de Tierra, into the Old City,
all a rampage of black shadows

on the faint blue cobblestone pleats.

# Cultural Stakes; or, How To Learn English as a Second Language

Wait on the corner of Isla Verde & Tartak
for your father to pull up in his Bronco.
Your mother will be right: he will not show up
at noon. At 12:20, you will recognize the horn,
its wail like an amplified conch,
but you will not recognize your father—
the gray stubble, the violent tan.
When he asks where you'd like to go,
say *the movies*, say *La Feria*, say *the moon*:
it won't matter. You will go to Duffy's.
When your father says, *We're only here for lunch*,
his voice will be as straightforward
as a sandwich menu. The bartender
will greet him like a cousin
in a language you cannot understand.
A stick of incense will burn slow
& its ashes will sprinkle into the tip jar.
Fruit will be rolling inside the slot machine;
darts will flash by like hubcaps. There will be
mirrors with bottles drawn inside them
& not a word of Spanish in the air.
When your father gives you a Coke
with two cherries in it, bite the stem
& bite the stem & swallow the juicy red wounds.
When he gives you a stack of quarters for pinball,
recall the chips he'd stack on the counter
after the casinos closed. Recall the night
your mother left him on the loose stitching of a chair,
the living room as silent as a funeral mass
where nobody stands to give the eulogy.
Don't ask him what compelled him
to call you today, eighteen months later,
& never admit that his absence
was a moist towel stuffed in your chest,
a constant fatigue of wanting. Don't tell him
what the nuns at school said about divorce,

that tin bruise on the spirit, & don't recount
your mother's remarriage to a man
who is as plain as his own mustache.
Your father will tell you many times
he is not perfect. There will be a sunset
on his cheek & a bonfire in his Adam's apple
& a coaster beneath his drink like a giant host,
the Scotch putting his tongue to sleep
like a pale stingray on the ocean floor.
When your mother asks what you did,
tell her you watched baseball all weekend
& bury your smoke-swamped shirts
in the bottom of the laundry. Every Friday,
she will watch you climb into that Bronco
& slide away till Sunday, your face
eclipsed by the tinted window's twilight.
At Duffy's, the women will be blonde
& they will seem as lonely as broken barstools.
When they speak to you, wait for your father
to translate, then reply to him in Spanish
& wait while he translates for them, & smile,
always smile. There will be something soulful
about this: the way your words become his
& his words become yours, as if the two languages
were shaking hands, casting one long shadow.
When your father brings a woman home, know
that laughter will leak through the doorframe,
that the body is an office always on the verge
of quiet. If she stays the night, the next morning
she might pull out a chair & gently say, *sit*
& this is how you will learn to concede
whenever a girl with sunlight digging into her cheek
taps your shoulder at the water fountain at school.
There, you will sit in the back row of catechism
& wait for the bell to trill its metal tongue.
You will stumble on the words of prayers
as if the short rope of your faith
was hindered by knots, as if religion was a field
with landmines scattered across. At Duffy's,

shed the red skin off the bull's-eye
with the lethal tips of your darts,
slide the smooth grain of the cue stick
over the wing of your thumb. Call all your shots.
Touch the chalk to your forehead
& trace a blue cross. When your father
begins to feed the slot machine's pout,
remind him to save a ten for the Drive Thru.
He will sit on a stool, pushing the *Bet* button
as if he believed that if he pushed it enough
he would fill with an air that could raise him.
When the language comes, it will be
as if it had always been inside you.
You will look at things & their names
will drip from your tongue. Abstractions
will be archived as events, & there will be
a history you can instantly shuffle through
whenever a word is uttered. For example,
*hustle* will be the night your father challenges
a stranger to beat you at darts. *Discretion*, the night
two of the blondes who cooked you breakfast
sit on stools on either side of you. *Impulse*
will happen over a rack of pool: your father will say
you have an invisible brother who is better than you
& you will spend the rest of your life competing
with a ghost. *Abandon* will be your first beer,
a squeezed lemon wedge inside the empty bottle.
*Independence* will be the moment you realize
the only hands reaching out to you belong to clocks.
*Irony*, you will come to understand, will be
when you ask your father about those expatriates:
who are they & what are they doing here,
so far from home, & why would anyone
ever leave the place where they were born?
*Fortune* will be every time your father hits
All-Fruits on the slot. *Innocence*
will come right after *Fortune*—every time
you say, *Let's quit while we're ahead*,
not knowing how far behind you really are.

# Cultural Stud

Who are you
tangled in the rap of Frenchies: Le Club,
plunking cigarettes backwards into your mouth,
your tongue a magic carpet
with one end tethered to the ground?
There is a pool table behind you
& two girls—topless—on their break,
cue shafts sashaying in & out
the smug gaps of their palms.
On stage, Extasis has more curves
than an ampersand, coiled
around the smooth metal pole,
barely an isthmus between floor & ceiling.
You know her waist is like the yellow line
on a bus, her nipples the knobs
for the tint of your dreams,
your mouth watering so much
the flood of want reroutes to your eyes.
You know you were born here.
This is Hato Rey, Puerto Rico,
& a Dominican waiter in a leather beret
insists you order another Scotch
because your ice has already melted.
There are traces of Breton
simmering inside the plush cushions
when Extasis abandons the stage
& you grab her arm
& tell her your heart is red Velcro
& she just *happened* to be
walking by. You tell her
the past, baby, is a sour grape
we learn not to bite.
This is Frenchies: Le Club
in Hato Rey, Puerto Rico,
& you were born here.
She is Colombian
& drinks White Russians.

She wants to be
an American citizen,
& you are tired of being
a graffittied wall
forgiving the humid caresses
of your vandals. You tell her
it's true: you have a token to feed
to the rusted turnstile of heaven,
but you have no WD-40
to make it turn. She is Colombian
& her lips stamp your cheek
like a passport, the aftertaste of Finlandia
napping under her tongue.
This is Hato Rey, Puerto Rico,
& you *have* to order another Scotch
because consumption
is the first policy of solitude.
The Dominican in the leather beret
tries to drown you in his shadow.
You know your busted wallet is empty.
You look to the girl for help
& she reminds you your ice has melted.
*How could it not?* you say
But she can't hear you. The bass
throbs. Strobes bulldoze the darkness.
Behind you, the 8-ball
drawn into the black hole of a pocket
trails little bullets of light.

# The Night Bernard Hopkins KO'ed Tito Trinidad

*Pittsburgh, PA*

Even before the snow    Pittsburgh
my throat    was flooded    with desert islands

your name    Pittsburgh    a see-saw
I want to tilt    towards the heavy end

your chimneys    are drooling
a toxic halo    Pittsburgh    hovers above you

in the bleached lid    of your sky
I wait    in a bed    of your trilliums

for the first    fraction    to wilt
look Pittsburgh    if you had a face    I would rip off

your beard    & if my heart    were a town
it would have    only one street

but a thousand    bridges    would bind it
I wear Pittsburgh    the dicey corsage    of your wind

on Forbes    walking home    Pittsburgh
a leaf on the sidewalk    is a dehydrated gill

& the flake of rust    that peels    off a car
Pittsburgh    is just

the flake of rust    that peels    off a car

# To Roberto Clemente

Like you, Roberto, I went from the town
of giants to the city of steel, where smoke
arcs over antennae & signals drown
in the Ohio, where the same broken
carburetors still sleep in cribs of mud
at the bottom. The people, still in love
with your arm, your bat-speed & speed, your broad
range at Forbes Field, the gold lace of your glove.
Do you miss the bridges, their fortified shadows,
the three rivers exhaling their vapor?
There is something to be said for this—how
every morning I open the paper
to the weather forecast page & scan for
Pittsburgh, though we don't live there anymore.

# Cultural Silence; or, How To Survive the Last American Colony

Stop at a *kiosko* in Luquillo, Puerto Rico.
Brush past a table of tourists, cameras hung like medals
from their sunburnt necks. The bartender
will move to the salsa that pours from a small red
radio, rust on the lone speaker like static. Behind him, a sign
will warn patrons: PROHIBIDO HABLAR DE POLITICA

& in front, everyone at the bar will be silent, as if politics
were the only thing anyone knows in Puerto Rico.
Outside, on the country road, a stray dog will not resign
himself to hunger as the tourists fork lobster medallions.
Above him, the branches of a Flamboyán will sag, red
as the blood of patriots you can't mention in this bar.

When a man proclaims *Cuba Libre*, notice the bartender
mixing Don Q & a Coke: how he ignores the politics,
how he squeezes a lemon & stares at you, his eyes redolent
of the O's in PROHIBIDO. You will want to order a *Puerto Rico
Libre*, though that is not a drink. Settle for a Medalla,
the national brew, its golden logo's design

suggestive of treasure. The tourists, who can't read the sign,
will begin to praise their expansionist president. The bartender
will say nothing as he flicks the can of Medalla
to make sure it's not frozen. To him, POLITICA
means only one language. You are a tri-colored bead, Puerto Rico,
in an island-necklace: ocean-blue annexation, Flamboyán-red

status quo, & mountain-green independence. You are a redundant
stalemate machine fueled by misperception. Know that no sign
will ever prohibit these thoughts. Every day in Puerto Rico,
you perch your arms like surrendered weapons atop the same bar;
every day you come home to the same stuffed politics
steaming on the table. When a tourist looks up from his medallion

& tosses an ice cube, the dog will bite it, that hollow medal
of charity, & bark for more. Here, you will want to speak of
    redemption.
Here, you will want to drop your own politics
like an egg crate. Don't. Instead, glance once more at the sign,
clutch your beer & drop two bills on the bar,
that mecca of sedatives: Bacardi, Barrelito, Palo Viejo, Ron Rico.

Drive off into rural Puerto Rico, sip your Medalla
& remember belief can never be barred. Plunge into the red
speech of the sun. Forget all the signs. Let cool be your politics.

David Hernandez

# Dysfunctional

Under the house the boy
saw the possum, creature
that doesn't know if it wants
to be a rat or a mole. Under
the house where the dark
lies flat on its square back
and the possum's eyes are ruby
in the flashlight's beam.
Playing dead or playing alive,
the boy not knowing which
until days later an olive stench
wafts into the kitchen window.
The boy again under the house,
nose pinched, dragging
the animal by its tail
into the light, into the weeded
yard, marveling how soon
it's greeted by a congregation
of flies. All day—
that's what he has to slingshot
pebbles into the carcass, to watch
the black knots scatter, settle
back on the fur, scatter again.
Until the evening hunkers down
to make the sun its chew toy.
Until father's jalopy
wheezes up the driveway
and mother crushes
a cigarette into her ashtray.
Before things begin to get ugly.

# Exploded View

After a gun is dismantled, the parts
weightless and numbered,
it's hard to believe it's harmful.
The hand spring is a bent
bobby pin, the hammer

a jigsaw piece. Assembled,
when the trigger spring nuzzles
against the trigger, the cylinder slips
into the pistol frame's squared hole,
it's another story.

In third period art class
Jason always drew head-on collisions,
toppled buildings, something
splintering lead, blown apart
with his No. 2. *Very good,*

our teacher would say.
*Very nice.* That summer
he pressed the barrel to his temple,
squeezed. I floated
through my days, head numb

with booze, forgetting
what I'd just learned: dates,
algebraic equations, the conjugation
of *vivir*—an eraser that swept
across memory's blackboard.

Only the theory of the origin
of the universe stayed with me,
that first explosion, so immense
the stars would always be hurtling
away from us.

# Wile E. Coyote Attains Nirvana

> It is neither by indulging in sensuous cravings and pleasures, nor by
> subjecting oneself to painful, unholy and unprofitable self-torture, one
> can achieve freedom from suffering and rebirth.
> —*from* The Four Noble Truths

No wonder after each plummet
down the canyon, the dust cloud
of smoke after each impact,
he's back again, reborn,
the same desire weighing
inside his brain like an anvil:
catch that bird. Again
with the blueprints, the calculations,
a package from the Acme Co.
of the latest gadgets. Shoes
with springs, shoes with rockets,
but nothing works. Again
the Road Runner escapes,
feathers smearing blue across the air.
Again the hungry coyote
finds himself in death's embrace,
a canon swiveling toward his head,
a boulder's shadow dilating
under his feet. Back
from the afterlife, he meditates
under a sandstone arch
and gets it: craving equals suffering.
The bulb of enlightenment
blazes over his head.
He hears the Road Runner across
the plain: beep-beep. Nothing.
No urge to grab the knife
and fork and run, no saliva
waterfalling from his mouth.
Just another sound in the desert
as if Pavlov's dog forgot
what that bell could do to his body.

# Dog with Elizabethan Collar

The contraption looks ridiculous:
a plastic ice cream cone
with a scoop of German Shepherd.
Who knows how bad he wants

to paw his left eye, half shut,
twitching in the sunlight?
Once I fractured my ankle,
untwisted a coat hanger to reach

an itch inside the narrow
tunnel of my cast. What joy
that bent wire brought,
what bliss. From the backseat

of his owner's jalopy, the dog
attempts to poke his funneled head
out the open window, rolled
three-quarters down, but the collar

knocks the glass, it clips
the window frame. Poor pooch,
he only wishes to dip his head outside
and feel the kiss of wind.

It brings me back to Jennifer,
cobalt-eyed and apple-scented
Jennifer, how every time I leaned
for her lips, she leaned away.

The traffic light flicks to green.
I press my foot down on the gas
and watch the dog miniaturize
in my rearview mirror

as I steer home to my wife,
my lovely breeze, who sails
into my life again and again
to kiss my lucky head.

# Ropes

I've swung on a tire roped to a branch,
hopped between two ropes arcing in the air.
I've felt the hot orange bite of a rope slithering

out of my fists, loved a girl whose braided hair
was a black rope hanging down her back,
long as the knotted rope of her spine.

And I've helped friends secure mattresses
to their cars with rope, and sensed our bind
slacken when they pulled away from the curb.

But now I'm thinking about the rope lassoed
around my waist, tugging me to the shower.
It's the same rope that drags me to work,

to supermarkets, Laundromats and car mechanics,
dinner parties, gas stations, banks, dentist chairs,
and waiting rooms. A constant wrenching

throughout my days. It's the same rope that falls
from my waist like an unloosened belt
when I am with you, and another rope,

one tethered from my body to yours,
pulls us together, slowly and mercifully.

# Suburban Story

When I was sixteen the sky disrobed
her blue dress and slipped into a black negligee.
I unfolded the phone number, called

the married woman whose husband
tattooed her body with his fists. Her dark voice
came through the receiver thick as honey,

moaning *Fuck me*. Moaning *That feels*
*so goooood*, a necklace of Os
she slowly lowered down her throat.

Downstairs my parents watched television.
I spilled and spilled, the sitcom's laugh track
audible behind my closed door.

How lonely I was that winter.
The moon was an ornament left behind.
And every morning, before my father

hurried off to work, he kissed
my mother by the kitchen window,
the sunlight varnishing their bodies gold.

## Whitman Dying

Walt in the sun, his forehead jeweled
with sweat, the horizon seesawing

until he topples, until he's planted
on a wheelchair. Then another stroke,

another dam erected inside his brain
before pneumonia steps in,

his lungs two Clydesdale horses
towing the heavy cargo of his breathing.

Then tuberculosis, his body
giving up now, throwing up its arms,

throwing in the towel. And his heart,
just look at it: corralled with lesions,

submerged in enough water
to keep tulips purple in their vase.

Now his deathbed, a waterbed,
little waves every time he coughs.

Say your good-byes. Make it quick—
Walt's on a raft, scooting out

into the sea, his beard a white sail
the wind won't leave alone.

## St. Mary's Hospital

This one cradles his broken arm and sings to it
a lullaby of moans. This one's all wrinkles and bones,
flopped over an armrest as if put to sleep.
This one gets up even though she says her legs
are numb, two bags filled with sand, and shuffles

toward the receptionist. My body's half ache,
half dizzy, a teaspoon of glass whenever I swallow.
Two hours until the intercom says my name.
I float beside my wife like a balloon tethered
to her wrist, through double-doors and into Room 1.

There's a gurney. I lie across it. The doctor
strolls in with his white coat, his white teeth,
and peers into the sick cave of my mouth.
*Tonsillitis*, he says. A nurse brings her pinprick,
the antibiotic's blue inferno. An unbeliever,

still I think of Jesus, a handful of mud in his palm
fluttering into wings. How I'd love to see him now,
robe skimming across the tiled floor, hands loaded
with healing. To witness a bone unbreak itself,
the elderly woman jolted back to good health,

her new heart an apple polished against his sleeve.
My throat cured, his touch a necklace I'd wear outside
where the healed are shellacking their bodies
with sunlight, where St. Mary's is vanishing
at the end of the lot, one skyward brick at a time.

## Man on an Island

By *island* I mean this narrow stretch of lawn
dividing the road, a boulder here and here,
little trees with trunks thick as broom handles.

By *man* I mean the one pushing the mower
with a red bandana wound around his head,
his face enameled in sweat. A wind-up toy,

he goes forward and back, the mower growling
before him chewing the grass. The sun
won't quit. It slams its heat against the world.

It makes chrome dazzle, the unshaded squint,
and broils this man on an island surrounded
not by water but tar, by cars gliding north-

and southbound, quick as sharks. Who knows
what his message in a bottle would be, what plea
on a scrolled wrapper in an empty Corona

lying in the gutter. Something about his rent,
his roof. Something about minimum wage.
A crude map of the city, an X where he works:

this island we drive by and drive by and drive by.

# Dear Spanish

For kicking you in the shin in kindergarten
this is what I get: how to say good-bye
to my grandfather on the telephone

an hour before a plane shuttles him to Chile.
Ninety-seven and two heart attacks, wanting
only to live out his days on the brown soil

of familiar terrain. Your lingo blooms
on his tongue. My tongue hobbles
around my mouth, dragging its bag of English.

Bless my voice so it knows more than
*estoy muy triste* and *ciao abuelito*. Bless it
so I could touch him in your language

and erase the seven flat states that keep me
from seeing once more the butterscotch
of his face. Now the static of a bad connection,

my tongue leaning on a tooth. Bless it before
the sky pulls him south, before we hang up.
We hang up. The empty kitchen hums

with the soundtrack of my blood running
in my ears, a language built on silence
where every word is swallowed instead of said.

Scott Inguito

# Guadalupe Beach

Say something
Give me hymning
If I have found my way
Back to you
On the floor
At table

The light line falls
Your face
If I have found
Sing back to me
In choirs of arms
Faces wooden
At table
Bread is fondness torn
Olives in the filling
Grape-stuffed empanadas
Pinched & curled
With brown hands

At meat
The breastbone aching
I've left the watching tea
Tried to listen
Culling a middle name
At your chest
If I have found my way
Back to you
Say something

I have a small dark lake
Inside me
The nude bridge
Populated by families
In blue nylon
Hold hands
Walk the shale road
To the dunes

Dull coats
Hunched over rails
Reeds strung with ducks
Nesting
Dull perceptions
Murder the thought
Of quitting

Drug the drearys
Mossy bottom dunes
Sand gets in this letter
Twitch
I am my own
'This Year's Model'
Won title
Old man in a hat
Paint a ladder
Between the two selves
We'll be fine friends
Hold up that halibut speared
Its white belly
Flashing in the sun
I'll pick you up
Some honey
I'll pick you up
Some glee
Straw hat and a can of peanuts
Won't buy a house
Near those eucalyptus trees
Grove of taco trucks
Quilted silver and blue
Morning fog and manure
This way this road
Is just dust houses
Faces and trucks

. . . . .

# Main Street

The air collects itself. Dunes. The tilled fields. Strawberries. Plump and salt air sweet. It's said that the French like Santa Maria Valley's berries. Boxes stacked high on muddy trucks rattle across roads. Bonita, Furukawa, and Minami Farms. Converted buses haul workers to the fields.

Manure wind. Stings the throat.

Ocean wind and muddy thigh-highs. Hands from Mexico make money and pass it to hands to build a better roof back in Morelia. The trucks, flatted to the brim, pull the twin Porta-Johns into the next field.

Lo Mejor de Jalisco. That's where the laborers eat. Campechana plato y refrescos y cervezas. Cuatro de Caminos.

Deepbend. Backbend. Cracks in the curl between the thumb and forefinger bleeding. White and dry.

The dog's name's Chicken. Been swatted on the rear too many times. Laps up the coffee that's been thrown on the ground.

Fields are corduroy. The telephone wires are bowed with black birds. The hawk circles and wobbles. Celery wind. Blade. Thigh-highs. Roofs are built.

# Papa George

Roosters. Fights on Saturday nights

In the direction of the water tower. Masatani's market. They got the egg noodles that Bud Wong's uses.

Chili Colorado at Guadalupe Café. The flour tortillas are fresh. Pats of butter.

Sting. Muy picoso.

Morning's mud. Lettuce, celery, broccoli.

Knives are romantic to a child.

A blunter. For the broccoli. They got special ones for the celery.

Chub blue handle. The blade is triangular. Short and oyster colored. Hairnets have yet to be improved at the packing plant. Both Grandmas work there.

Forklift operators are god-like.

Booby. Filipino/Mexican biker. Two thick black braids down his back. Shaped like an apple. His pants always hanging down. Didn't have an ass.

Batman calling Robin. Come in Robin. Dad goofing on the intercom at the refrigeration plant.

Union. Good work. The ground is rich and the irrigation is plentiful. Sea air gets in the strawberries. You can raise two kids on a lift driver's pay.

Coors. Leroy Park. 25 cents a can to the "Uncles." My hand aches from the ice.

Strawberry wind. Celery wind. Broccoli wind.

Hooded Mexicans, Pilipinos, Japanese. Mud walk. Dust walk. And some like me.
Mixed.

Chickens over grills the size of a truck bed. And garlic bread.

# Parade

Diamond lamp
Burnt over cream
Little dance before
A bad tune

Come again to black books
Ink over horizon
Those are fine-ass cops
Cruising the café
Tell me more, tell me shame

Look at me over dinner
Light up a door
Lash a cross
I'm not fallow

Want to talk shambles
Laughter, chairs
Cigarettes, recovery
Bring knees together
Shamble up the pine
Give us a whip
Come trilling
Away on calendar

Forest green nylon
With a white zipper
A ruddy heart
Served under lights
At a gas station
A broken open
Papier-mâché maraca
Made with a burnt bulb
Break it for the parade

The Compton Sounders
Who follow the Caballeros
White and brown longhorns

And clowns
Blackness
Fetishization
Fishnets
Sound me, candy

Breathless out of a plastic
Horn, white boots
Men ride horses
Miss Congeniality waves
And buckets of Coors
Sounders wake us
I want to kiss you

Good-bye cousin
The truck idles
Tent a stake
Under canopy
Dirt
Fruit grove burns
In the sun
While Papas burn
Rail ties in memory
Pick fruit, retread tires
And fix Volvos

Father's shoulders
Burdened by chickens, grease
Black dogs bite
The grandchildren
No feeble mustache
Proud
Crying is much to bear
In Spanish
A priest ties a knot
Who's he talking about
Cousin
At the bottom of the lake
I am camping

Bring the sandwiches
Salt
Gold locks will
Shine
I hope
That they write
But that they speak
Of the chick raised
On the playground
Taken by the hawk
At recess
Perched upon
The phone pole
Devilish sweet tear

Carrying a painting
A hawk nailed
A blackbird nesting
Outside the art building
At community college
Screeching bleeding
Dropped a drawing
Dead blackbird
Best not to rot
Lonely on an empty
Paint locker

Flooding furious
Hold me
A chair bleats
So be near
Hold knees closer
Pink chambray binding
The collar
Three gone years
Bad the bye, bye
Song to city
Red needle
Keeps moving

Blue water I leave you
Take care janitor sir
Give the residents
Hugs from me
I can no longer
Sit with them
For pictures
And prayer circles
I will remember
The healed sores
On your hands
That punched trees in paradise

## Bats Trace Their Droppings Painting Words

Bats trace their droppings painting words. A bit of bump and loss, Therese holding the reins of oxen, light fur movements along the ridge of the back. Ritual hours lodge themselves in the grotto, beautiful soft shores absence of she. Lips in troughs with love hidden among necklaces of lime fruit. We push away thighs, bellies, fleeces, begging to be brushed. One touch interiorizes crimson Pauline! Ghost solutions are solutions, twisted, tangled mass of airsucking out amorous stains in suits. A little copper scratching clues away silence and is lost.

On a glass box uncertain mixing of blood. Stir the azure noisily. Feign a chill, drink patiently the melancholy hours.

I retrieved the tight flesh-colored dress from the salon. A chaotic letter was pinned to the left strap. 'It was only a dream. Witness the useless splendor in the hard mirror of the sequins. Love, Sunflower' I'm waiting for a reaction from my limbs, thighs, something to call me back into the dress, something murmuring another fabric, a voice clinging to the cut of a body, hips and bones and delivered figures and all the little lies. Each gold shoulder a façade bearing witness to the Maranatha Blvd. Blotter of bird shit. French-tipped day.

## I Have Been Resisting, Due to Bad Knees, 'Falling into the Work of the Living'

> As we struggle towards life, it is thru our inventions that we offend the dead: as they in their time offended.
> —*Robert Duncan,* Letters

I have been resisting, due to bad knees, 'falling into the work of the living' as Duncan writes in his letters. I fear I don't know to offend the dead. That to offend, that is our true business. A friend has written so close, so pressed through that membrane between living and dead. My reticence; misplaced reverence? I am often more than guilty, complicit. Do you "shift your miserable bones," due to my stumbling?

> All dead bodies radiate prayers, ancestral emanations to insure the continuity of semen, blood, of spirit.
> —*Robert Duncan,* Letters

To desire correspondences, to look for them, to see them. And then the shock of their sensations dissipating. And then? Duncan experiences a correspondence to Adam in writing:

> It is Adam whose signature fell into a multitude. With what fear I have discovered Your signature in mine, as Your body is in mine.
> —*Robert Duncan,* Letters

We are in our time to offend. This is our lineage. "Signature in mine" of the hand. "As Your body is in mine," of the body. Lineage, a correspondence. But are we not *in* time, in a continual flux of dissipating correspondences? And what to do? Say? Resurrect the image of a correspondence as Duncan does? Contrast, re-construct rather, a shape, an empty work, a monument to correspondence? To now take the vapor of dissipation and fashion droplets, or "freshets" Duncan writes, of that cloud of canvas, paper, will. Is it all merely vapor, as Ecclesiastes writes? I am not vapor. She is not vapor. The living are not vapor. The dead, their prayers, are the vapor we breathe, the dust we pull from our fingernails, the ash on our knees. In, not of, mixed in, not around, the dead are here and we give another voicing, mixing in with them. This is not the same correspondence. Co-respondents. Mixed respondents. Hello. How are you? I am fine. Lick my ear.

Sheryl Luna

# Her Back, My Bridge

She sat blush-cheeked, straight-backed & beautiful,
thin-waisted & tearless at the window when she first came.
A crumbling brick sill beneath small elbows. Brown eyes

glisten, wish to receive dresses, jewels from American GI's.
The street below smelling of dead things, outhouses. Her flowered
red-green dress, panty hose rolled over bony knees. As a girl

she could dance; she'd scrub poverty with Ajax to find peace.
She stuffed her cheeks with Mexican food—*Las Tinas*, big vats
of pintos, rice. Riding the Santa Fe boxcars to pick onions

in fields. Thirteen siblings screaming, sleeping. She was broken
early by a boy. Found herself on red knees, taken in an alley.
And the tears, did they come? Her eyes forever worried

by the sun. Has she seen trees sway wind, were clouds and sky
ever blue-green? Could she kill that boy, now a man,
with a cast-iron pan? Chihuahita's buildings red and gray

beneath the loneliest polluted sun. She's too old
to clean now. The state's lady comes twice a week
to scrub her frail back. They won't scratch

her back *hard* enough, won't dance her age away.
She's pissed. Wrestling's her favorite thing,
*Pícale, Pícale*, she screams poking the screen

with a pencil. Her shoes once rubbed ankles
raw, yet she's sway and swing, her voice a dove's call—
Jesus, Jesus. She told me one spring of the dove's hopeful

mourning in the fields. She's breathing thin now, her veins
too thick, her bones hollow, her left eye glaucoma-
silver. A bedroom mirror covered with pictures,

my own ten-year old American face rosy and cheered.
She tells me, "I'm ready to die." Her favorite song,
"La Puerta Negra." The Black Door.

"You've got to be strong in this life—
*mijita*." Here I am singing the unsung positive capability
of the desert, how weeds grow orange wildflowers.

## Slow Dancing with Frank Pérez

I called him fish-lips, Frank was all bones,
dark. His knees sunk in at the sides.
You could mistake him for a runner.
When he kissed me, he barely opened
his mouth. The tip of his tongue peeped
into my mouth, two fish sucking rubbery
lips. Fumbling and leaping like salmon
into a glorious world, its incalculable
madness and beauty still fresh.
Our breastless, peckless hurried sway.
My arches ached from moving tip-toed.
Our oafish knees and the lyrics
hummed in meaningless pulses and tones.
I remember the floor moving,
the ceiling aflame in colors. Each pain,
each trope blooms now to real meaning.
Frank never made it to twenty. He died
in a parachute accident, a broken young
body. I still see his black curls, eyes
two pits of dark innocence. And life is like this,
hurried and awkward; the way pride swells
and need takes over, all weary desire.
The way those lost speak through an old song
that lives *duende* or heart and steam, knows
what it means to touch. Smooth songs
sting something more than sexy, each word
swells to images, implodes in icons.
Memory does this, helps us live
through all the cutting borders,
the aches of our slow return to bungling
knees and bony hips.

# Learning to Speak

I forgot how to speak. The old man with a gray
beard eyed me, waiting for Spanish.

Years of English rumbled something absent, forgotten.
The Tigua Indian Village, men at the corner bench eating

tamales. Indoors, tables with white Formica,
floor-tiles peeling. In the steam of cilantro and tomato

children sit cross-legged and sip caldo de res.
Men smoke afterward in faded jeans and t-shirts lightly rise

around their pecs in the wind. It is how home is all
that's left in the end. The way we all return forever exiled.

History in mud houses and shady river-trees. Canal water
drifts. Children poke crawdads with dry branches. I spoke

Spanish broken, tongue-heavy. I was once too proud
to speak Spanish in the barrio. He waits for my voice.

His eyes generations. My brown skin a scandal on the hard streets
of El Paso. But, everyone loves a resurrection. Mauricio on a red

motor bike; Bob, a green-eyed white war hero, spits tobacco.
The sunlit desert and its gold light falling upon us. *Quiero*

*aprender español*, I whisper. He smiles. Blue hills
in the distance sharpen in an old elegance; the wind
hushes itself after howling the silences.

# Two Girls from Juarez

Two girls from Juarez hesitantly step toward my desk.
"Ms.," one says with a paperback of Plath's *Ariel*

corners folded and coffee stained. "Was she white
or black?" One with over-dyed red hair and black

roots announces, "She was prejudiced!"
I am now questioning my life in a desert; questioning

as lightning rips the sky like an instant of daylight
in the hard black lake of night. In Plath's "Daddy"

a black man bites a woman's heart, and all the wit
and the wordplay between darkness and light shrugs.

I am bitten. The girls want to know
about Plath's gasps, about her white

eyes in darkness. One wears an electronic
bracelet around her ankle.

The other's cheeks red with too much rouge.
I imagine they live nights dangerously

in an Oldsmobile near the Rio Grande,
that they love for real and they love to love.

I smile at them with no answer. I lost answers
long ago and the faces of my colleagues grew ghost-like

and words fell away and the poetry cancer came
like a priest for the sacrifice.

# Poesía de Maquiladora

I am swept into a sadness, still
and unspeakable in sterile rooms where
men might as well wear white coats
and drink my breath from stethoscopes.

They were so happy to show us
the habits of locusts, drain blood
into plastic bags of their manufacturing.
Tell us, Latina, was it what they
assumed it was, broken language,
poetry of a lesser nature, a wound?

The way my brown knees
slammed hard in the fall
from what was left of grace.

My eyes shrunk to slits, my only
salvation came in the flight of grackles,
the way the moon swelled, striped
with red-orange light.

It has rained more this spring.
I am sick of having to watch what I say.
The grackles have beaten the songs down
with their desperate caws.
The tree branches scream, too, now.

The most intelligent doctors walk
through their patients. Assume a sickness.
My mind has pleated itself
in a veil of shadows.
My body is fading
back to an invisible border.

# Pity the Drowned Horses

It is one of those nights when you fall back into childhood
like the breeze gentle against your half-quiet ears.

The tall Italian cypress still giant to your small eyes,
the moon lopsided—still, holy, mysterious.

The clothesline droops now and the height of the line,
once a Herculean reach, is only an arm's length away.

Your feet easily plant themselves on the ground and no longer
gleefully dangle while arms stretch sinewy & young.

The stars hum still & blessed. You carry the cracked hose
to water the drying tree, & the dead grass sings a silent hymn,

the water's dribble makes you want to cry, not because the pipes
are dry like your grandmother's bones, but because the sky

is still, yet moves like the night you turned seven. Here,
the dry garden hose brings tears to your eyes, and you weep

your insignificance. The dead neighbor's white Chevy truck
parked in the same spot for years is gargantuan, yet invisible.

Mr. Tellez, try to remember his round face, his broad back
in a white t-shirt watering the pink and white oleanders.

Were they imagined? Was his face so unimportant? The truck
looms undisturbed and heavy. The highway buzzes where desert

once sat calmly. Cars replaced screaming children, bicycles
and the holy ritual of running through the sands native,

dark thighs sweating in what seemed an eternal sun.
And what do we care for the smallness of another? It's our

own shame, the way palms clench or eyes dart fearfully,
the way we learn gossip in shadow, talk ourselves

into believing god is listening because we are afraid,
the shadow on your pale cheek is darkened like the blue

lake of night. All you can do is eye the slow gilded stars,
the black lake of sky, memory above the forty-foot trees

through a broken branch. The moon waltzes with the veil
of night clouds and finally water gushes and the tree's roots drink

the last waters, the first waters, holy waters brought down from sky,
and you still may think of Moses and mist like you did when you

were twelve, and may still imagine god's waters crashing down
on the heads of your enemies, yet pity the drowned horses.

# An Atheist Learns to Pray

Maybe you found the moon sun-lit in black
space or gazed at Saturn's blue-red-gold prism.
Slow warmth in an empty universe, light
became your daily bread, night a starry
sacrifice. The way darkness paints and blots
havoc. We always return to beauty
after the abyss, bruised and cold, learning
that a rose open to May is unburdened.
Why not swing our hips and sway as leaves chime
to dawn. One learns from children, a dog's thick
ribbed breath, the rise and fall of night. Even
when slandered, one drinks water and the sky.
Blessed be the way caught among showers,
the sun later rising like a man listening to god.

# The Colt

The sky glowed its red burning, and the damp
      air smelled of mulch, and the earth called
itself up inside of me like a smoggy song.
      The colt's belly round like a donkey's.
Wet and frizzled brown hair trotting

behind a brown-white spotted mare,
      proud in its tall-legged towering.
Thin-ribbed dogs running through traffic.
      We call far into the distances between us.
Wind brushes my cheek in a cold need.

All things, drawn to one
      another like the flippant tail of a colt
in a barren field where the flat bed
      of an eighteen wheeler rusts and the tractor
rests upon its fat tires, and the black eyes

of birds, the wings of crows flutter
      with a deep-throated call of hunger, want
like a cool shadow over the broken
      neighborhood. Chickens like the fretted
hard strums of electric guitars run wired

through the yard, squawking then beating the sky.
      And there stood a child like an old god,
running, nipping at the larger horses' legs,
      wild with the birthing, fresh before the earth,
the wind nothing but its very breath.

Carl Marcum

# We Drove Some Chevys

*'72 Chevelle Malibu*

Sometimes a Chevy's just a Chevy:
one you can take to the river,
and (no surprise) the river is dry,

like the song you just thought of,
it's stuck in your head all the way to St. Mary's
and just past the interstate, the Santa Cruz is dry.

Sometimes a Chevy's not just a Chevy
but instead a '72 Chevelle—eight cylinders,
gray as a ghost, babymoons waxing full

in harsh streetlight. The summer
monsoon tastes green and hot, the desert
in your mouth. A hunch, a thought:
*the river is running, brown as a boot.*

*'64 Nova Convertible*

Red, like a marching band, like a bandera,
the kind of red that looks best with green:
it flashed past you down Oracle Road,
stock as the showroom floor, turned
your head like a schoolgirl in a miniskirt.
There are only metaphors to explain
how it was headed south and you were
headed north, the hot wind at your back.
The top down, and driving that machine,
his moustache thin as a wire, sunglasses
on—*perfecto*—was the happiest vato
you've ever seen, the wind in his hair,
the sun entangling the windshield,
exploding the light: a minute-long blind spot.

### '74 Camaro Z-28

Rene bought it brand new. Blue as the ocean
in his dreams. The yellow and white racing
stripe down both sides, fast as a shoplifter.
What better car for the Levy's store detective?

That Camino ran nearly on machismo
alone, thick as Rene's beard.
How the gringitas loved his dark, good
looks—a Mexican Travolta. My mother's

youngest brother, Rene kept me and my primos
in line without saying a word; he had a stare
that scared you enough to behave, like the stories
I'd hear about my tata. Once, he caught me

and Johnny in the Camaro's bucket seats,
shifting the tranny, playing with the lights
and estereo—what we knew of freedom
was the open road and an open Coors.

"Qué están haciendo?" Rene's voice asked
from behind us like a stone. "We were just playing . . . "
Rene looked right through us. My mother said he
smiled only when we walked away.

### '67 Impala Super Sport

Mayate green, a June bug dance.
That loco worked overtime, worked
double time—we're talking Christmas
and Easter—stocking the aisles

by the pallet load. Got him a promotion
and a paint job. Green and gold
like the silken mayates we'd catch
on mesquite bark when the summer

clouds would roil angry in
the Rincons. The three coats of paint

cost a grand apiece, and the wheels?
Olvídate. He got a deal on those.

He went on dayshift and wears
a tie: assistant grocery manager.
He keeps those aisles as straight
as that car. Too bad it's up for sale.

He went and knocked-up his novia
celebrating the promotion with a case
of Coors and that long back seat.
He keeps telling me about her long

black, black hair and her breath
on his ear, sweet as tequila.
She's a nice girl and all,
pero, man to give up that car?

## '69 Nova

It belonged to my Nino Ramón, originally.
A gift to him from my mother for his departure
to college. She was working then, making good
money counting money for Capin's Department Store.

Ramón installed the dual exhaust
that rattled the windows from the street,
and the sticker in the back window, the fat
circle of an American flag. He grew his hair

long and didn't go to Vietnam. That car,
blue as lightning crackling across the black
monsoon-summer sky, streaking from Nogales
along the dark summer highway.

Years later, my father took the Nova
back and forth from the air base. The blue
lightning blanched and oxidized by the
jealous summer sun. So my father

stripped the paint down to silvered metal
and primered her white as a sheet—dull
and matte as an old horse, a ghost horse.
I was fifteen, and Tom and I had our eyes

and plans on that car. But the three gears
and eight cylinders were deemed too much
—though I suspect my father
lost the title to a full house against his two-pair.

Mine and Tom's "Deathmobile" never carried
us anywhere, not to the cinema, or stale class-
rooms, or to watch the Pantano fill and run,
flash-flooded—lightning bluing our eyes.

*'79 Monte Carlo*

That car was ugly, a big steel
box, but it looked good as a lowrider.
Almost anything looks good
as a lowrider. The Monte Carlo's
one saving grace: the seats
swivel outward like an office chair.

There's an old joke
that asks why we drive so low
to the ground—it makes it easier
to pick lettuce, *ese*. Why else
would we put a hydraulic suspension
on a car? Go pick your own
fucking lettuce. And we'll pick
up the pretty girls, cruise the boulevard,
and celebrate this life—ripe with summer.

*'82 El Camino*

It was Tío Cosme's last quixotic
wish that we load his coffin
in the bed of the El Camino

to drive him to the grave,
draped with the American flag
he'd served all his life.

That El Camino, sliding tan
and immaculate through the streets
of Nogales. Everyone crossed

themselves as Cosme motored by.
Rene, in the driver's seat,
taking his brother for one last ride.

The air, so hot and heavy in May,
and the seven guns flaring their three-
toned salute, and the flag to my tía,

a dark triangle of midnight.
And I couldn't, for anything,
remember the last time it rained.


## Barrio Brisbane Gives Witness

The sidewalk: some neighborhood kids have angled
        wide board against cinder block
                to ramp up their rollerblades
and have begun to record the breadth
        of their bravery with red, white, green
                chalk slashes. Two boys and a girl.

She out-jumps her counterparts each time
        and they grudgingly lay her green stripe
                down past their own and come faster
to the ramp each time—thrill
        of gravity defied for however many
                seconds: the muscle-clench and wince

of pleasure. They can see in her brown eyes
        that she won't decide if she will let

either of them win. They're eleven,
maybe twelve, and before the summer
is out she will kiss both these boys.
And how they've begun to admire

her longer, more graceful leaps of faith
in her own brown body. How they look like
they'd never look away as she shakes out
black hair from under her helmet.
How they've suddenly fathomed a want
deeper than any wrapped birthday.

And they see it in each other. And hate
each other for it. And like this, they learn
to conspire. And while they lie in their
beds in houses next door to one another,
they both rise in the unhappy dark,
ripe with orange blossom and gaze across

the street—confused and never before so alone.
*Alejandra, Alejandra*, each time sweeter
and less forgiven across their lips.
And she skates through their sun-dried
dreams, *Alejandra, Alejandra*.
And they know vacation will come

for them both, and they become more aware
than ever of those delineated days
—June, July. Joe knows Tony
will leave for a week south to visit
his sunny grandmother. Tony knows
Joe has to go to Silver City as soon

as he returns. And like this,
they become sullen, absorbed in the
delirious glue of model cars, the binary
graphics that entangle their hours—*Alejandra, Alejandra*.
While Tony is away, Joe kisses
Alejandra in the dusk, popsicles melting

in their hands, the sidewalks spotted sticky
     and skates still on their feet. Tony brings
          Alejandra back a present: Shamu snow globe.
Tony kisses Alejandra beside the pond in the park
     while koi look on, murmuring their algae secrets.
          Then Alejandra returns to Arizona

after summering with her abuelos. And the boys sit together
     on the silent steps of Hilltop Market
          watching the last days of August sink
in the miserable sky. *Cherry popsicle.*
     *Blazing fish. Alejandra, Alejandra,*
          abject in their mouths.

## First Snow

November's commotion settles on my
shoulders like good fortune. I'm still delighted
by the white idea that's begun to fill
the city: accumulation and decree
—specific under my boot. Remember us,
Mother? You, postpartum, sister asleep
in another room. I had you to myself
again. We stood against the cold and foreign
light of a Utah winter window;
the snow falling hours on end and my
childhood delight with the constant flurry.
Our faces reflected in spider-frosted
panes, and I could see you fill with sorrow
as each astonishing flake tilted through
our view. I know now, as the city
forgets itself in the chaos and grace
of ice, how you yearned south—missing the desert
the way I watch out this window missing
you now, with each amazing star.

# Notes from the Art Institute

Zapata, *José Clemente Orozco, oil on canvas, 1930*

If I'd grown from the same branch
as Juanito back on Bantam Drive:

*I'm fucking serious, whiteboy.*

I'd like to think that *that*
is what I'd say seconds
before singing a switchblade
into existence:

> *I'm fucking serious.*
> *Whiteboy.*
> *Knife.*

But as it is, I'm not bothered in this crowd . . .
their backs turned to me, mine to them.
Hopper's *Nighthawks* draws their famous
attention, not this minor Mexican muralist . . .

. . . And Zapata looms massive in the doorway,
red, brown, white, and silhouette. Knife
and his eye, a broken moon. And the foreground
cowers beneath him.

> *Fucking serious.*

Zapata, that brown boot
in your doorway.

> *Knife.*

His eyes, somber under his sombrero's shade, the flat
gaze of gesso. His hands, obscured—am I to assume
his knife? Assume my fist in the cold flash
of metal—honed edge of have to:

> *Whiteboy.*

Give me wide berth through the Pre-Columbian exhibit.
I know the Toltecs, the Aztecs, the Mayans
believed in human rites and the blades that enforce them.

María Meléndez

# Remedio

Let go your keys, let go your gun,
let go your good pen and your rings,
let your wolf mask go
and kiss good-bye
your goddess figurine.

There is a time to grip
your talismans,

a time to strip yourself of them.

Spirit and flesh
will have sometimes had enough

of go-betweens—

A refastening
of our noses and our ears

onto our soul

can only be accomplished
in the company of master exemplars.

Take wolves, each with a soul full of scents:

asperine willow leaves
and damp earth, willow-rooted.

At the end of summer, a wolf's soul hears

cottonwood catkin's
long trajectory down an ageless azimuth,

feels, in her inner ear,

myriad shifts of air
        as the tufty seeds ride twilit rays
                and glow as we imagine all
                        eternal things to glow.

A remedy for when you've lost your sense
of Spirit in the world,

a simple spell for home lycanthropy:

>Smell the new season,
>acrid, tensed to grow
>in budding wolf willow,
>and feel the heat recede
>from a moose's corpse—then
>*recuerda esta loba.*

*Recuerda* . . . from the Spanish *recordar*
which is at root not remember or re-mind,

but pass back through the heart—

>let her pass back through your heart again,
>this wolf.

## In Biruté's Camp

Suppose God is looking for a good
            piece, who could be you with that bare
                        strip of scalp parting your long hair,
            braided loose and looped up in the swamp heat,
sweat curling around your small, bristly eyebrows,
            your hands gleaming with juice and pulp
                        as you hammer fruit on the feeding platform.

            That strange orangutan,
the human-raised one called Pan-gan,
            who throws men off the dock
                        like an overzealous baptizer, may
            be a god and here he comes
                        padding side to side onto your platform in the swamp.

If he curves the ridiculous length of his
tendon-riddled arms around your waist
and wrestles you down to the wooden boards,
    scream—he'sbitingyouhe'stryingtokillyou—no,
he's pushing up your skirt—

                become limp below the waist and make your torso
            a flexible branch for him to squeeze
                as he swivels from one world to the next;
            (now he is calm and deliberate,

                            now his eyes roll upward)—

            When he finally moves off
                    the feeding platform and into the trees,
                        rise into this loss, which is relief:
            his seed will shimmer out of you, unrecognized.

## Nude Sonnet

When studied apart from chickadees and crooked paths, you seem
    built of

                                concave lines
        (scoop of shoulder blades, curving pectoral base,
        crescent canoe of pubic hair hung from pelvic bones,
        soft swoop of glutes, furrowed muscles along the spine);
I'm guilty of examining your form uncomplimented, unembraced—
sink-fixing, baby-washing, goddamn hockey-watching man,
tolerant, tolerant man, why don't you ever say I'm beautiful, but then,
why don't I ever say that you are? I'm checking skin at the boniest
    place
of your ankle, and even there it's smooth; consulting the stubborn
worry lines bowed across your forehead, divining the asterisk of hair,
*size of a silver dollar (cupped between your collar bones), querying
    the air

along the part (can you believe it) in your armpit to learn if you were
    born
on the same stained sheets that I was; but any guilt you bear is sown
in hair sprouting like a trail of needle grass to your navel: beautiful
    man,

                        unscoutable meander, my own.

# Tonacacihuatl: Lady of Our Flesh

*Sacramento Valley*

Fragrance of the rain in her breath. The dampness
at the back of her knees smells like rain also.
She appears with a shining crow the color of cinnabar,
and a mark at her shoulder blades displays the same crow.

Poison has made her throat lovely. For that poison,
praise is chanted in heat-meters making triple-digit noise.
Part of her has the form of a tule stem, and that form
she can absorb, if she wants it hidden. And it is hidden!

How many spirits she's twin to, and how long she'll last in this world,
are secrets stashed in the rattle
of corn ears, in the coils
of venomous snakes.

Thirteen mirrors spangle her dress. For those sun-round mirrors,
praises are chanted by thirteen thousand red-legged hoppers.
At noon, she steps out of a culvert and collides with the naked light,
and her fever is an affliction known as August.

So she is, Lady of Our Flesh, who is what is.
Is she not here, who is our mother?
Huffing, with matted hair, she stamps a shovel blade
to begin a small grave.

# An Illustrated Guide to Things Unseen

Here's the turquoise cheek
of a fathead minnow,
netted from the camo-tint
    can't-ever-see-what's-in-it creek;
   dropped on your palm, its glowing lilac thread
  of spine bisects your lifeline.

        Here's the spirit of a rhododendron garden
         (slurp slurp slurp it's all for show)
        impersonating "Redwood Grove" in an arboretum.

  Here: two pipevine swallowtails,
     crazy with the indigo smell of each other,
  spiraling past a grinning red cat
    in the ivy, past a bearded man
      on a picnic bench who's leaving
       a short-haired woman, here's
        anger fastening over her
         like an acorn cap.

Here's a rapist's habitat
between snowberry bushes
and live oak shadows.

        Here's a whole night
    heron rookery in a cottonwood,
   and here's a woman feeding stuffing
   to the ducks; she has bitten the tip
  of her baby's little finger.

Here, the reburied bones
of the First Woman exhumed during
construction of a Performing Arts center—

        Here's a poisonous oleander,
       concealing a well (and not so well,
           after all)
       from hypothetical polluter-terrorists.

For those of you suffering
from absence of riverflow,
    here's bowlegged Waterman
        stuck in the ground ("vacuum breaker");
    within his corroded metal
     swish and rattle of water tumble,
        unlappable; its curling rhythm
     mimics the undercurrent of silence
     in the waterway you're trying to love,
        the unyielding laminar surface
        that's breaking your heart.

## A Secret Between Lady Poets

How we two lust after news
        from the Peterson case,
wife & child pulled from the Bay,
        dripping wire & weeds & rec boat refuse—
talk of the Coffin Birth, coroner's slang
        for a dead child's delivery
from an already deceased mother; submerged
        as they were for months, we
picture all tissues softened and elegantly
        torn like damp newspaper,
baby's lips ragged and fluttering like some lilting
        anemone, both of them suffused
by the faint light found in lurid
        aquarium displays—it's a fact
your husband's just been stashed,
        ashy and silent, in the baby blue
urn on your piano. Too bad—he would've enjoyed
        the defendant's fish story:
"I wasn't boating in order to dispose of a body,
        I was trolling for sturgeon. With lures."

"Oh sure!" Walt would've chuckled sarcastically,
        knowing that tackle's for bass or muskie.
Me, I'm here for the night, on leave
        from mothering wifely duties,
making a mourning visit to you, teacher, friend,
        mother-in-tangled-language, because
we've got to keep an eye out together for whatever
        the hell happens next. You've been breathing
under the water of grief, I've been sliding through the marsh
        of my own maturation,
swaying between believing, unbelieving,
        what was early beaten into me
about my built-in moral defect, naughty mollusk.
        If ingesting the gore of the world with you
is a favor, it's the least I can do.
        So we sip our Court T.V.
all night, eat green grapes so engorged
        they're almost see-through.
Desperation and loneliness lap outside
        your full, square house,
waves that rise to douse us with desire
        for higher lunacy.
Up on the main floor, with God's
        chilly wind in our faces
we can't be bothered with fear anymore,
        we're gaining access
to the carving hand of the Holy,
        we're slowly exploding
into nun-ness, and moonlight
        slanting through the blinds
tracks right through us, translucent as mist
        rising from the surface of sorrow.
We're sorceresses now, source and mouth, all delta,
        pure, salty confluence
of the world's terrible, originary forces;
        the remains of our lost lives
curdle and foam on the shore, display
        the power of decay to begin
the parturition required

to unfasten dead familial bonds.
We slip into the continuum
of women destroyed or nearly destroyed,
women who surface in frightening forms
and wreak their stories on shores.

## Has it been whispered all along?

She lifted death from Poudre River,
curled it up in her arms—no
body (she arrived too late), but death
remained like flood debris,
so she carried it until the weight became
fiber in the bolls of her shoulders;

you know the facts—
her lover guiding a raft of tourists
down Pineview Falls,
the raft flipping, and the rescue
of all the customers by other boaters,
the way he waved off the safety rope,
floated conscious for a quarter mile,
stood up at last in the shallows
and took a few steps before collapsing
from a broken neck—

how his friend called to tell her,
and she screamed *stop joking*—how
she dreamed of him that night,
walking naked towards her,
muscles twisting like water
in his lean form.

A tree knows the whole story—
manzanita, red and gray wood
intertwined, alive and dead,
knows she made his death

a skeletal ladder, knows death rode
her every twist and growing knot
while she rose toward the reeling
of the sky—

Maybe death is the wildest movement of all,
and in this arid range we inhabit
there is moisture to be found at the boundary
between the two woods.

Maybe you can follow the orange-waisted ants
into the tiny space left
between living and dead;
maybe what looks like a line of demarcation
is actually an alcove,
a feast of hidden droplets—

Carolina Monsivais

## Writing the Circle of My Life
## by Remembering My Great-Grandmother

In Mexico, earth is reopened
so loved ones will be buried
together and their stories won't
be forgotten

Many sow stories like seeds,
which grow against the loss
of memory

Nana is buried in our family
collective grave along with
stories of relatives she never
told me about

When I write, I fall into gaps
where her stories
should be

I am fighting now
for the memory of Nana,
searching for reasons why
she and her daughters

all chose to weave cocoons
around themselves using strings
of silence

# What I Remember about Almost Drowning
# in a Lake Somewhere in Kentucky

My brother, sitting on a boulder near
the middle of the lake. I followed him,

unaware of sudden dips and hills along
the lake bed. I drifted down into the water,

looked up, and wondered what had happened.
Hands pulled me out, air poured over my

face. My father breathed it into my mouth,
expelling the water from my body. He turned

my head. I could see my mother's clothes wrapped
wet around her swelling abdomen. She still reassures

me that my brother climbed down from the boulder
to see how I was. I have no memory of that

moment nor of any other moment where his voice
should've broken through moments submerged

in stillness. It's the last one of my father, still
in his boots drenched from jumping in after me.

# Early Signs

Soaking in the sadness of others is leaving my bones porous.
That is what my doctor told me as he prescribed medication
to help me sleep and medication to fill the hollow spaces

forming. The bone shielding my head remains hard and defiant.
It makes me sit up and write on anything I can find,
including my prescription to patch myself up, until I fall asleep.

# How the Eye Works

Contours bend light reflecting off faces.
      Backdrops vary, reclining chair in office
hospital examination table, classrooms,
      detention centers, shelters, and churches.

Rays pierce cornea with images upside
      down. The spot behind the eye like film
burns the image and sends it through
      the optic nerve. The mind reverses

the image and stores it. Sanctuary,
      the bridge between short term and
permanent. The image develops
      details not seen only heard. Backdrops

become a waiting room with an uncle
      asking for birth control, a mother leaving
early for work, the father turning the knob,
      a knife under the throat with promises

of love. Light off roads bends and renders
      everything that shouldn't be ordinary.

# Phone Intake

I didn't even glance inside the small pink bag
before tossing it out. Policy after so many days,
and it has been weeks.

She calls looking for it.

The name: I shuffle through faces until hers
becomes clear, jaw unhinged, skin covered
in grated ashy sores.

The first I interviewed alone.

Brenda, my trainer reminded me of procedure—
forms with specific questions—good matches
need to be assessed.

She needed a place to stay until doctors could
realign her jaw. Saliva oozed from her mouth.

I remember wanting to hand her a towel,
Brenda reminded me no one would be able
to use it again. She was given a box of tissues
and her own trash can.

I'm sorry, we no longer have your bag.

She and her boyfriend count out their days in pills,
she needs her ID for follow up and medication.

We threw it away.

When she asks, what she is supposed to do now,
I stumble over responses, read numbers listed
near the phone.

Before hanging up she asks,
What kind of a fucked up place is this?

## The Interpreter

Habitually, he holds his neck within his hands and squeezes. Captures truths within his throat that slip through thick and round as coins leaving weight and the taste of dirty copper on the back of his tongue. Today, he feels ready and requests that I, his caseworker, help him render words he can say in either English or Spanglish, decipherable to his mother's fluent Spanish. We meet in the group room within the boys' shelter where he was placed after he and a friend were found high too many times. Clean, he quelled the clamoring with his hands hinged at the wrists and fingers clasped to the sides of his neck. The session's narrative forks, then fragments during pauses for breath and translation. He begins with recent reddish-purple trails along his neck, traces them to the afternoon alone with his brother's friend. He'd staggered home and said nothing, just showered, then watched the blood running down his leg swirl with piss and water. He ends with the scar above his brow from the night his father pulled him from the shower and beat him after he'd in turn touched another boy whose father demanded jail or retribution. The two men shook hands over his body wet and clumped like a towel dropped on the sidewalk. He begs his mother to forgive him, to find a way to love him. His mother turns to me, and I pause momentarily before nodding. She reaches out to him.

## Granada

Our first time buying groceries
together we begin with fruit—
Pomegranates—for which
I never seem to find
the word in Spanish
stored away unused or replaced
never matched in English.
You ask the grocer Manuel.
He blinks back at this pair
of pochos in produce.
"Granada," he says.

After our steady begging,
she'd pluck one—
a tree inside the garden,
the high concrete walls.
Susana, her duck, waddled
through the graveyard
of statues retired from
guarding the front door.
Cantinflas's chipped faces
smiled in unison at an array
of animals fading to white.
My grandmother would break
open the thick skin
revealing membranes
that looked like beehives
nestling capsules of red flesh
around seeds: reminders
of her bedroom, the only room
in her house with color
that matched her favorite
lipstick. She'd cross the lines
of her mouth, hoping lips
would appear larger, fuller.
She'd feed me stories
about my father, my grandfather
that turned out later
not to be true.

# Seasons of Writing

Sometimes the clouds
in my mind fill up
and at first
drop like a drizzle
gently covering
the page in a mist
then become a torrential
downpour, violently
saturating it.
My words flow through
the lines and form
rivers that flood
over banks
until I slip on them.

Sometimes the clouds disappear
and leave my mind dry.
The open sky unleashes
a blaze to scorch
the page
which cracks
beneath my pen.
But I can feel
the steam as it rises,
ignites my senses
and slowly fills
my mind once again.

# From Houston Back to El Paso

I decided
when my sister told me
everything was fine,
even though she'd packed
the cabinets with boxes
of baking soda and jugs of vinegar
after she explained once again
to our grandmother why
she no longer uses cancer-causing
chemicals to clean the house
when my grandmother asked
for the I don't even remember how many times
where the dishwashing liquid was while
contemplating the extra filter
for the filtered water and my sister
even though she said everything was fine
continued her explanation with a vow
to live without electricity then
asked my grandmother
if she'd ever used a washboard
and I noticed that the coffee we usually
sipped slow as we talked about everything
seemed tasteless
since the chemotherapy had stolen
the taste from my mother's tongue
and I realized when my mother spoke
of the recent death
of her friend like she was somewhere else,
more concerned with how much she hated
the way she looked in a wig,
that it was time to come home.

# The Funeral

That place inside my chest
I'd been trying to revive

stiffened when I saw her face.
That place I'm embarrassed

to admit exists, strummed
by ideas like first kisses

and early correspondences.
It seemed so important having

felt numb for some time.
When I saw her face,

unrecognizable from my
recollections of her in groups

with other girls laughing while
they discussed what is healthy

and what is not in relationships,
inside my chest it all seemed

to stiffen, then cease. I noticed
the makeup unable to conceal

ashy blotches on her forehead
and the different stories jumbled

in my head. Only the gun
in her hand, her boyfriend

close, and that she was thirteen
were certain.

Adela Najarro

## San Francisco

My great-grandmother taught my mother to read using chalk
    and a black slate in León, where adobe brick
        buildings are white-washed Spaniards

and history. We brought with us red and blue macaws, panthers,
    and crocodiles. Tooling up and down
        Dolores Street hills, my Papi rode

a bicycle delivering Lela's *nacatamales*. Back and forth
    from a clock tower at the end of Market Street,
        a renovated 1919 streetcar,

transplanted from Milan, works tourist dollars. Advertisements
    from the late sixties posted behind
        True View Plexiglas. I can't read a word

of the European Italian glitz, deep blue of the Mediterranean
    and a Coca-Cola, but there is a warm blanket
        on a wooden bench and a leather

hand hook. Above a Cuban restaurant, where waiters serve
    black bean hummus and chocolate croissants,
        hangs the gay pride flag alongside

a Direct TV satellite dish. Gabby walks to school, Pokémon
    cards in his pocket, Sanchez Street. I work
        in the kitchen with my Lela. Mariposa Avenue,

Valencia Street, Camino Real are added to *masa*. Homemade
    tortillas puff into sweetness. I'm not
        one-third Irish, one-half German,

and two parts English with a little Cherokee thrown in,
    but last night I couldn't translate the word "hinge"
        on every door that opens and closes

to clouds beyond four walls. An old lady, perhaps Cambodian,
    Vietnamese, Korean, something of her own,
        hurries off the 31 Stockton while

my tía Teresa double-parks in front of the *mercados* on 24<sup>th</sup> street
*para los quesos y los chiles* in the back room. One
whiff and the world is not so small.


## My Mother, Sex, and Dating

Though she was sexy with her stockings
and silk slips, she didn't

think it was good. Seven years after leaving
my father she wore a satin bra

under a gold and black knit sweater
which I could see right through.

I pouted and exclaimed,
"You can't go out in that!"

My good mother now tells me
I should hold off on sex, though

I'm divorced and in my thirties.
After Elizabeth's wedding reception

at the Richland Pub, we all
went back to her house in the woods

and I slept with a man who wanted
only to hold me. My mother tells of dancing

all night with a soldier or man in a tie.
She must know how the heart

gets lost once a palm is placed, open-faced
upon another palm, how the fingers

curl under and how the neck pleads
for a kiss, and I think John

knew this, too. That's why he confessed
that he didn't love me and why we didn't

do anything else. I thought it was understandable
for my husband not to want me

to wear make-up and to have all my clothes
three sizes too big. My pants were held up

by one of his old belts. I tucked
the extra leather through a loop, almost around

to the back. We both wanted for me
to be a good mother. She swears

she went home after breakfast at the diner,
offering a thank you and a fake phone

number, and I have to believe my mother.


## Throughout New York City

Emotional instability demands a new pair of shoes
and a leopard-print coat. All the men are beautiful glass

houses. Desire struts down Fifth Avenue, past Gucci and Chanel,
throwing blocks while shaking the rattle. I have been behaving

badly chasing after a man in a blue wool coat who lisps
in Spanish and smiles with a crooked eye. A late night

phone rings and rings, while in the morning
dreams morph a black crow's claws onto my left

ankle, a scavenger picking pieces from the not dead yet.
I should leave this city and practice patience. If only

to sit outside and wait for the temperature to cool as light
elongates through the shadows of a maple tree. Those damn-near-

perfect leaves in cadence with the wind, as the wind
goes round and round the earth's circumference. Vibrant.

Volatile. Never ending. An unnamable interior ooze settles
for a minute with my modern-day gaucho on a New York subway,

the F train, or maybe the E, and then I am terrified,
not of what might be or what should be, or the socially

constructed this and that of how a woman
should act concerning desire, but of electrified confusion

that cracks open a thunderstorm's loud boom while children
kick and scream through nature's chaotic dance.

We find shelter under an aluminum awning over a five-story
parking garage and by running down subway

mid-summer sauna steps to another connection,
another train. All holds still

with permission to touch a knee, hip, shoulder,
a slight seductive brushing

back and forth as we sit on pre-fabricated easy-to-clean
subway seats. I could fall

into forgetting, but I cannot shut down
the box cutter blade steady

in that woman's hand, or ignore that we all clutch
bags slung crisscrossed over the shoulder, the possible

intrusion from the outside, an actuality. Our bodies,
moist and pliable, wait for the one who seeks

to calm or release or turn-the-table on that same interior
ooze and find refuge, a palm in the dark. In the lilt

of so many bodies swaying with the continual rocking,
there is only more of ourselves. We rush to leave

tiles falling from turn-of-the-century walls, the steel
gurneys and iron pillars erect under the city above.

# Between Two Languages

*Misericordia* translates to mercy,
as in God have mercy on our souls.
*Ten piedad*, pity us the poor and suffering,
the lost and broken. Have mercy. *Ten piedad*.
*Misericordia*, a compassionate
forgiveness, carries within
*miseria*, misery, the stifled cry
on a midnight bus to nowhere,
and yes, the hunger, a starless night's
piercing howl, the shadows within shadows
under a freeway overpass, the rage
that God might be laughing, or even
worse, silent, gone, a passing hallucination.
Our nerve-wracked bodies tremble.
Our eyes have trouble peering into night.
Let us hope for more than can possibly be.
*Señor, ten misericordia de nosotros.*
And if we are made in the image of God,
then we can begin heading toward
the ultimate zero, the void
that is not empty, forgive ourselves,
and remember the three
seconds when we caught a glimpse
of someone else's stifling cry.
Compassion, then *miseria*, our own
misery intensified by the discordant
ringing of some other life. Our ultimate
separation. Our bodies intolerably
unable to halt the cacophonous
clamor of unanswered prayers.
But nevertheless we must try
for no reason at all. Once more,
*Señor, ten misericordia de nosotros,*
forgive us for what we cannot do.

# Playing around César Vallejo

The day I was born
God conched his mighty roar
into Khrushchev's ear.

Dandelions bloomed yellow
and continued to fall
away, countless airborne,
and a very young boy
sat down to a bowl of chickens
scratching the yard.

Few know the leopard-print
pajamas I found on sale and that
I've withstood stars withered
into a faint echo, the pulpy mass
of a tomato
cut open, sliced, and slivered.

The day I was born
God found his sense of humor
and whispered a dirty joke
into my grandmother's ear.

Oil heated in a pan,
kernels of rice crackling before
water, and she forgot the brush
taken to my mother's legs, the welts
of anger when a bullfrog
let loose his mighty tongue.

Let's go to the Dragon River
and order moo shu pork rolled
with plum sauce. Did you wake
in love this morning?  Never forget
a warm December and the cold
water deep in a lake,
August, September.

The day I was born
God was feeling much better.

What is the proper location
for a box of rusty nails
or those squirrels,
those damn squirrels again
sitting on a fence. Who knows
what you know and what is true.

I think the earth is in league
with red-tail sparrows, maple trees,
and even the stench of tar, wet and fluid;
all laughing as we sit
confused and mourning January's
overcast sky, the death of an oriole
frozen in ice.

And yes, César, light is inexhaustible
as well as shadow,
and it is the Mystery, the vast space
of what is unable to be said
that is kicking,
kicking us upside the head.

## My Mother's High Heel Shoes

      A fat man in white. A polished stone floor. Marble or granite
cool in the hot sun. Circular tables.     Chairs. Umbrellas.
      A patio deck.
Inside the cabana, at the counter, I ordered a hamburger.

      In Nicaragua?     Maybe it was a soda

in a highball glass with a cherry. I do not have to ask
for money. I am part of the black sand, fine silt, and seaside sparrow.

      The sun drapes freckles across my mother's shoulders.
Ponoloya, a beach in Nicaragua. She is seventeen and pretty.
      I lost the 8x10 glossy.
Each eyelash curved. An ivory cheek. Joan Crawford lips.

      I think I took it        to school for a class

project on family history and autobiography. In the second drawer
of her dresser, a satin slip the size of a Mead college-ruled notebook.

      How close can I get to the first bikini on Ponoloya?
Saturday at three o'clock old movies re-run on KTTV, Channel 11.
      Clark Gable. Claudette Colbert.
A shapely leg in a silk stocking extends for a ride

      to champagne       and elegant parties.

Cummerbunds. Gold taffeta. Who does my mother kiss on a blanket
as Abuelita scolds her with a look that keeps hands in view?

      My mother spots a picture in a Paris magazine or one
de Los Estados Unidos and asks the seamstress to make her one just
   like it.
      Probably blue.
It would have covered her belly button but exposed two inches of ribs

      below the bosom.      Esther Williams

pulls back her hair and raises one arm before submersion.
On an overcast day we head toward Huntington Beach.

      The piping tube of a seaweed frond stuck in a castle turret.
Half moon slivers.    Crushed shells.
      Pebbles in sand.
My father, my brother, and I are added to a shoebox.

Urayoán Noel

## Ballade of a Boy

He grew up on an island that was torn
From pages of an in-flight magazine,
The local cynics said he had been born
Before authorities could intervene;
In fact, the cops concluded he was clean
And finally agreed to let him go.
The next two decades he would spend unseen,
Attempting to forget and to forego.

His mother dressed him early on in scorn,
His father went for liver failure green,
I do not mean to make him sound forlorn,
In many ways he was a normal teen:
He'd oversleep, make trouble, and careen
From job to job—Mc'D's to Texaco
To Mexico and back through Abilene!
Could I have guessed how he would end up? No.

All I know is that he learned to mourn,
Looking at once despondent and serene,
If every human life were shot as porn
His would be the scrapped seduction scene.
I saw him one last time by the porch screen.
He did not speak, but seemed to wave hello.
It was as if his eyes were trying to glean
A shuffle in the stillness, an echo.

Don't ask me what it's all supposed to mean,
That last good-bye was many years ago
And so much else has happened in between.
Perhaps the in-between is all we know.

# Kool Logic

The Cultural Logic of Late Capitalism; *Frederic Jameson*

**1**

I hope this finds you in good health
(Or at least gainfully employed).
We're here to discuss the hologram-self
In the era of the void.

Some say modern man is hollow,
Others say it's a condition
Called "postmodern." Do you follow?
Could this use some exposition?

**2**

O.K. See the common graves
Rotting in the ancient cities?
The fast food? The porous borders?
The ambiguous sexualities?

The debt-bludgeoned ethnicities?
The wars of chemical roses?
Cash flows from Utopian rivers
And the market never closes!
            *"This is the kool logic*
            *Of late capitalism."*

**3**

In the Prozac marketplaces
People hoard new modes of leisure;
Love has been deregulated:
Plastic breasts! Prosthetics! Seizures!

In the suburbs neighbors mourn
The death drive of their libidos,
Late summers full of soft porn,
Stolen Wonder Bras, torn Speedos.
            *"This is the kool logic*
            *Of late capitalism."*

**4**

You can consume what you please:
From work music to new age;
Ricky Martin and John Cage
Are touring the Basque Pyrenees;

You can sing your songs of peace
(Pop! Punk! Folk! Tribal! Assorted!)
But the violence will not cease,
Hate's fetus can't be aborted!
     *"This is the kool logic*
     *Of late capitalism."*

**5**

Macrobiotic-cybernetic-
Fiber-optic folderol!
Neo-gothic supermodels!
Satellites and virtual malls!

Vegan power lunch grand slams!
Word elites! Money-go-rounds!
Free will or free (pillow?) shams
In the global shantytown?
     *"This the kool logic*
     *Of late capitalism."*

**6**

NBFTA, Mercosur, Hamas!
DVDs and open mikes!
Watercross and motocross!
SUVs and mountain bikes!

Trailer parks! Gated communities!
High-rise ghettoes and favelas!
Acquired diplomatic immunities!
Self-help prophets! Braille novelas!

Mexico, Miami, Río!
Euro-Disney, Bollywood!
Dell, Intel, Taco Bell, Geo!
Stanford post-docs in da hood!

I'll stop fronting pedagogical . . .
One last question (extra credit):
This kool logic ain't too logical
But it's still "kool." Do you get it?!
　　*"This is the kool logic*
　　*Of late capitalism."*

# Barrio Speedwagon Blues

## I

There's melting pots sofriendo
Masitas de muchedumbre
Y tengo la mala costumbre
Del que sonríe sufriendo;
So I stare outside my window
At the rats who pay their dues
Down abandoned avenues;
Varios diarios relicarios
De vecindarios precarios . . .
Barrio Speedwagon Blues!

## II

I don't mind the daily walk,
De nuevo nursing the nightmare,
I'm happy just going nowhere,
Fast-track dreams in laugh-track shock,
I wear the street's scar, just like Prufrock,
In the crater of my shoes,
In the sunset's purple bruise,
Under streetlamps sin que alumbre
Mi cómica pesadumbre . . .
Barrio Speedwagon Blues!

### III

I've learned all my civics lessons
In this republic of deadpan,
Emptied out my mental bedpan
With Zen and antidepressants;
Now I'm stuck-in-convalescence
Y se me quiebra la cruz,
Y me acuerdo when we'd cruise
Down the coast, nursing home injuries,
Singing our song of lost centuries:
Barrio Speedwagon Blues!

### IV

I'm too old to take a ride
In a rented chrome machine
Down the freeways and ravines
Hurling my pain to the tides;
Now my autism collides
With the headlines on the news
And my lovers say I snooze
En depresión atmosférica,
But I still dream of America . . .
Barrio Speedwagon Blues!

### V

Esta ciudad es un empate
Entre alcaldes billonarios
Y activistas solidarios
Atop a corporate mattress;
But I'd never knock the Rat Race
'Cause my blood cannot refuse
Its internal revenues
De burgués y de atorrante
Y el que la sepa que cante:
Barrio Speedwagon Blues!

**VI**

Esta canción no se acaba;
Gimme a sec and I'll finish it,
I'll spew out some funny shit,
Metaliterary baba;
So drop your joint and your java,
Stop scribbling those curlicues
Parce que maintenant j'accuse . . . !
Slumming days away like Dreyfus:
Why does all this feel so lifeless?
Barrio Speedwagon Blues!

## Death and Taxes

The housewives laugh at what they can't avoid:
In single file, buckling one by one
Under the weight of the late summer sun,
They drop their bags, they twitch and are destroyed.
He hears a voice (there is a bust of Freud
Carved on the mountainside). He tucks the gun
Under his rented beard and starts to run.
("The housewives laugh at what they can't avoid.")
Like she-bears fettered to a rusted moon
They crawl across the parking lot and shed
Tearblood. The office park is closing soon.
Night falls. The neighborhood buries its dead
And changes channels—Zap! Ah, the purity
Of death and taxes and Social Security.

## Cave Painter Blues

Before there was a self there was a cyborg
Cave painter, a hand whose dimly lit marquee
Of bloody parchments served the purpose of TV:
Advertising life-on-Earth, in morgue

Light. Squinting, he distilled the everlasting
Impression of leaf-blown river rapid roar
(And the blunt rock, what was it there for?);
The prehistory channel was broadcasting

His signal-tower graffiti, the timeless chronicle
Of the disgruntled marshland frog, the dodo's chant,
The brooding bear, and the hypnotic ant,
The memory, the wound, the smudge, the mineral.

Today he cleans his brush and bides for time
Selling T-shirts outside the Guggenheim.

Deborah Parédez

## Stella

in the year of my birth
lightning struck the roof—
electricity's axe split the house apart—
our family running out in all directions

I made my way toward school, the only brown girl
cast against the glare of German faces,
my brown skin bruised
by thrown rock, thrust boot heel
my brown skin darkened
by the ruler's strikes against Spanish

throughout it all 'Ama and 'Apa
armed us against subsequent strikes—
gathered every fraying quilt,
split flour sack, fringed shawl—
and covered all the mirrors in the house

at the first sound of thunderous rumble
they would move through each room
unfurling fabrics
covering anything, they said,
that might draw in the lightning,
anything that might reflect the light

## Mobile, Alabama, 1963

In the seasons following your father's death,
your brother began his insidious visits to your bed
and your mother became a seamstress, pushed
the parlor furniture aside, crowding all available space
with metal racks adorned with their own strange fruit:
starched cotton frocks, waves of jersey, crinolines

rustling like whispering ladies of the Junior League
anxious for the next occasion. You
took to them, joined their ranks,
in among the hanged at eight years old
you preferred these sheathes, vacant
semblances of womanhood—you
would rather be a dress, you thought,
easily unbound from the body each evening,
you would rather be a dress
because it was too much to be a girl
unwound night after night unwound
as a bolt of fabric, yard by yard
stripped measured cut and bound
into unseemly pattern.

Yes, to be a simple dress
on the rack in the house of a widow and her children
during the seasons when outside—just beyond
the rows of spooled thread, the seams began their unraveling—
just beyond the parlor whirring with its dogged machines—just

beyond: the early gatherings for the long march toward freedom.

## The Gift, Uruguay, 1970

Flora in the year before the coup
the yellow truck skulking just
behind her at every turn

her *novio* Tomás a biologist in love
with the living world
with every last organism

each week wooing her with a gift
last week the slug on moist brick
this week a handful of beetles

next week through the hills
the couple in flight
pursuing reluctant bullfrog

their bodies upon capture
shaken by laughter and fatigue
frog clasped in trembling grasp

Tomás offering her his final gift
yellow truck lurking
and in the moment of transfer

the small animal seizing its chance
leaping free from quivering hold
beyond the borders of their sight

## Sonnet for Rilke in February

Winter in Oaxaca where weak against
El Norte's brutal elements—the ground
broken open only for the dead—I
cower in the *zócalo*, at a loss
for words, outrun by the elusive verse
weeping at the scent of gardenias,
their strength these hours outweighing my own.
Thoughts turned to Rilke, steadying himself
like stripped birch against February's blows
harkening to Orpheus in that one
"single breathless act of obedience."
Oh, to possess Rilke's faith, his courage
to take root, await the miraculous
blooms—the bees stirred and rising to their tasks.

# The Fire

The night Tony decided to end it all,
bathing his head and limbs in gasoline
and igniting himself into effigy
in the third floor dressing room of the theatre,
roaring and tumbling down the stairs
like the damned on their way to hell,
you were working late in the scene shop,
goggles on, all safety procedures met,
guiding plywood through table saw's teeth.

The night Tony seared the shop's doorframe
with the stench of flesh in flames and the
screams pouring from the O once his mouth now
melting away, you stayed calm, moved
quickly, took all the necessary precautions,
you knew what to do to save his life
and your own and you did it and then you drove home,
pulled two six-packs from the fridge,
hauled them to the back porch, tilted your face
toward the heavens and drank
until every spark of light blazing from
the stars went dark, you drank
until your body could hold nothing more
and then you pissed right there in the yard, your bladder
now emptied of its fire.

That night you learned the danger of a body
burning and pleading and staggering towards you
so that years later when I, a bright girl, ablaze
and reckless, rushed to embrace you,
you did only what you knew best to do:
you stayed calm, moved quickly,
took all the necessary precautions,
snuffed out every ember,
saved yourself.

# The Trumpets Raised

*for Gary Rafferty*

The dead are marching before us today
as they usually do, bearing the grace
of an unrehearsed high school marching band,
their tune difficult to carry.

We are standing near enough
to one another for you to notice
I am straining to see—
there are so many bodies among us—
so you reach your hands out toward me,
the gesture bearing me up
the way the father will lift the child
on his shoulders at the parade
so that she may join the line of witnesses.

And this time when I see Girardo
drowning in liquor, slurring curses
until the space around him turns
charred village, this time his body
surrendering to supine twists,
his tongue swelling
as the seizures capsize his sleep,

this time
in the drowning, the burning, the choking
I see the steady procession,
the trumpets raised
to announce the return
of a man surviving
the war.

# Avocados

*after Vietnam*

The war went on in the house
well into the eighties,
skulked from room to room
more sinister than gas leak or thief.

Those were hard years:
the refrigerator home to nothing
more than half-empty salsa jars,
stale bread, six-packs of Schlitz,
avocados gone black and tender
as charred flesh.

The father going for days
eating only avocado sandwiches,
working knife through rough skin
and silky meat until the slick dark center
was all that remained.

Then precise and diligent as any surgeon
he would begin his work: pierce
the gleaming pits—four toothpicks each—
suspend them in jars half-filled with water
lining the windowsill above the sink.

His rituals with crusts of bread,
dulled kitchen knife, rotting fruit
were displays of exquisite rationing:
he knew how to take it and take it
as the jungle takes monsoon,
grows leaves, conceals the enemy.

Daily the girl studied his martial skills,
but she could not make a life of it as he had:
like the pits hanging nose down in water,
she refused to unfold her roots for the planting.

# The Early March

The mornings after each encounter
there is no swift return:
instead the northward walk towards ninety-sixth street
the inevitable, huddled wait for the cross-town bus
face turned eastward against the rising sun—
the lumbering approach—
compression of brakes and bodies
in a symphony of squeal and chime
then the transfer to the Broadway local
submerged beneath the *bachata* beats of Washington Heights
until the train's eventual ascent near the island's edge
its steady climb from the depths like those first reptiles
ascending from the sea in cautious crawl
their newly shaped bodies glistening
like these early March morning sidewalks
glistening as their icy scales are shed.

This morning, already giving way
to afternoon, there is no rush:
only this last descent from the risen platform at 225th
this steady climb up the paved slopes of Marble Hill—
*clave* of keys keeping rhythm—
only the assurance offered
by these weeping eaves
relinquishing their winter weight
over the alcoves of door after unlocked door.

## *Nóstos*

At long last
nearly through my entire repertoire
voice hoarse from relentless lament
I have worked my charm, worn down the gods
convinced them to grant me my return
to her, this girl-child, my former self
this shadow of braids and poncho fringe.

On the long walk toward the way out
she follows my voice through the darkness.
There is so much I wish to say to her:
that the rhythms of epic exploit and departure
will not be the only ones that will move her;
that there will be others who will chart their course
through tempestuous seas for her rescue.

I sing her this hymn and as we near the end
I turn toward her. I know the rules
know this gesture will force our parting.
I have brought her as far as I can.
And in my final glance, I shift
my body's shadow so the light
flashes briefly across her brow—

her face a forsythia branch breaking
winter's spell with its blooms.

Emmy Pérez

# Solstice

*the americas*

War in sun country
Lights water with orphans.

Braids sawed off. As if arms.

Pray for snow, and thistle
Blooms purple along

Roads. Amaranth grows
Beyond the harvest.

                    *

Morning sky: more meadow
Than metal. A clear-eyed orphan

With stars on her tongue,

Hiding her siblings
In the sun glow.

A soldier knows a kiss
Won't open that mouth.

# Irrigation

### I
In empty acequia
her body
ripped easily:
a husk
shucked in wind.
Her arms, her legs,
bent like tassel silks.

## II

Winter floods
into cotton fields.
The whole town
thigh-deep
in the irrigation ditch,
stabbing catfish
with large pitchforks.
And still, she insists
on the machete,
firm in her hand,
chopping pears
from the cactus
thinking: *this*
is the sweetest red.

## III

She will grow bones
the way a shark
grows teeth.

# When Evening Becomes Stellar

Orchid sky seeps through
our window veiled with branches.

The day heals itself in amethyst
fever, entangled limbs.

Iridescent corona,
keep safe your ivory

light. My calf's tusks
are attached to the skull

of the sun. Ancestors
run under our bellies

like clans of mule deer
sinking into sky's velvet.

There is the constant beat
of prowler's paws on the desert

drum, a watering hole
to find, there are pairs of teats

gorging with white. In the cover
of bosque and penstemon, a she

beast is born, unafraid:
with trembling legs.

## One Morning

Yellow pines    No ever    no green    except
where stems brown needles green    I walk

on the wooden train    The fall's water you swam in
one cold morning    What you braved    That ice

path    A horse fence    Where fences are horses
with long hair    I braid the tale the fall of stables

Four paws touch dirt    stirring
a flirt of sky a bundle of rare    You bundle

into stables    I open with sandy tongue
taste the grain of barkwater

I look at myself in
a mirror of weather

Rain trenzas    Dirt cups us    We drink

& spin like tornillos    A swallow's nest    like an adobe
tornado    Shit & mud & feathers & forming pitchfork claws

Eggshells gone    We rest in the ocean smalls
the pink throat

The back door is also the front    The only
smoke hole    Feathers rise
& we follow


## Swimming

She could have her baby while climbing a jacaranda or walking up
        stairs.
He would bounce down each branch, each step—his bones still soft
        and
rolling into the city street intact.

The baby grows straight up, and she can only grow out. He likes to
        eat,
thinking one day he will break through the atmosphere and be closer
        to
God.

The mother swims in the Pacific each summer because there she feels
weightless. She wants to dive deeper, but her ears pop and pressure
        builds
in her head if she kicks too far down.

The sun licks her dry when she stretches naked on sand. She rolls in
crushed rocks, crushed shells, lets the waves crush her, licks salt off
        her
lips. Here she can breathe freely without slashing two slits in her
        neck.

Such stars in the sky, such stars in the ocean.

# La Aurora

One having missed seeing dawn/separation . . .
—*Leslie Scalapino*

*One having missed seeing dawn/separation* reaches back into REM-state, closes eyes to hear white-winged doves. Images in black space seep rust red, la aurora's arrival turning the shades, a ficus scroll wetting itself to avoid the flame. A woman loves an unidentifiable being, presence, above a mass of caves, navels where *Loltun-Loltun-Loltun* resounds when fists strike failed stalactites. Separation from set into rise, the nocturnal sleeping, bright-eyed in a sky half imagined. Set. Rise. Rise. Set. The hours in between, 2012, predictions or prophecies, apocalypses or a flock of lips colliding—pursuing—climbing before day is served on a severed endeavor. A feathered coat, a watering hole, a pirate boat, carry off what was our unconscious, what was the power of the body to heal itself in flight.

# Ars Poetica

The pain in the rooster's cry. My anguish, not his. He is pre-storm glimpsing electricity's gypsum, positioning without knives. We all want to catch light, drink water without thinking about toads. At the call of thunder, spadefeet emerge from hibernation and enter the acequia's bamboo ears. Without solstice would we fall?

I want geography—to know it like driftwood knows it. Offer new shapes for the macaw's tongue in the fashion of precipitation. "Ahh! Ahh!" he says as a school girl pushes "Polly want a cracker" like a veteran paleta vendor. "Ahh! Ahh! Ahh!" he replies until "Whazz up!" surfaces on the momentum of his pendulum.

Zoo verbs—envision turquoise feathers above forest canopies; close a cold eye and see dandelion seedheads along San Elizario's canal. And fear the stroke that controls the tongue. Dementia as mentor and magenta the cue stick. Halos break apart, splitting nuclei, neutrons bouncing behind closed eyes until the whole state glows ember. We need another's skin to suck until dawn.

Open window shades and feel the sun. To know it is to lack it and lick it. We're lucky to shower every day like starfish pyrotechnics.

*Drink, Drive, Go to jail.* If only latchkey highway signs persuaded rain. The river fantasized by maquiladoras: a humble mail-order bride, astral tassel around her waist, a rush of fool's trove at indigenous prices. *Drive friendly. The Texas way.* Tomato splats on *Welcome to New Mexico* merge with dusk in Santa Teresa, Anapra's sister. Anapra, Chihuahua, just a tocaya and patrol Bronco away. Calling all agents! Erase a day's work of watering dust devil hedges and swim in the Río Bravo with snowy egrets and colonia residents.

And Dear, I love you the way Budweisers love caliche arroyos, the way reptiles scale burrows and sore-eye poppies make boys cry. And globemallow pinwheels, my little horned lizards, please guard this roost made of mud, as stellate hairs and amphibian bleating woo a monsoon from this toxic evening.

## History of Silence

When did you begin?

        Beauty
Intentionally buried.

Don't comment on screaming.
It didn't happen—
        Did it happen?

Maybe they didn't think
We'd hear. Of course
They knew we'd fear it.
Silence is memory,

Black space in the mind's violent eye.
Silence is choice.

Don't comment on memory.
The screaming
Didn't happen.
Silence

To erase, Latin *erasus*
From to scratch
To scrape
More at rodent to gnaw
Akin to
Sanskrit *radati* he gnaws
Etymology
Silentium
13th century
Absence
Of mention
Oblivion
Oblivisci
To forget
The fact or condition
Of forgetting
Having forgotten
The condition
       Or state of
Being forgotten
Or unknown.

Corn is our history.
Why is it called an ear?
An ear hears and after
Eaten the cob remains and remains
And remains.

Sugar cane, shiny reeds.
Who would count the inches
Between sections of guitars,
Staff for notes, staff
For tuning circles, frets,

Shadows in between
Or the sweetness contained inside
Telephone wires.
Let's talk
Like marionettes.
Little leather boots
Against pregnant stomach.
Is the uterus
Pregnant or the woman?
Spiritbody within the spirit
Or body.
Can the spirit control anything?

Fret
Middle English,
To devour, fret,
From Old English *fretan* to devour;
Akin to Old High German *frezzan* to devour, *ezzan* to eat.
Date: 12th century
Transitive senses
*To eat or gnaw into, corrode, fray, rub, chaff, to cause to suffer*
*emotional strain, vex. To pass time as in fretting. Agitate, ripple, wear,*
*to become agitated. Grate.*

Hands of the puppeteer
Atop the wood cross
Handle, an instrument
To drive, and the little hook
To hang it up
After playing extinct
Will hang like a good
Fall. I could
Fall in love with
The operator's forearms.

A row of soldiers.
A row of bodies.
This is my row.
Definition: *Row:*
*Date: 1746*
*: a noisy disturbance or quarrel.*

Fresh corn rows
With silk tassels
I can be tender too
White and flattened
On a stone.
My sisters' bones.
Where are they?
Stalls in pupils
Between rows
In the desert
Dilating
Bullets
Mother
Corn
Utterance. History
Of indigenous.
The murdered women's pictures
Millions of self-portraits.

*Note*: based on definitions from *Merriam-Webster's Dictionary*

Paul Martinez Pompa

# How to Hear Chicago

Here a spirit must yell
to be heard yet a bullet

need only whisper to make
its point—sometimes I imagine

you right before your death
with an entire city in your ears.

# After Words

Even the sidewalk aches. Burnt out street
lights bow down as if ashamed. Somehow

the fat oak on the corner dodged the bullets.
So did the bus-stop bench no one ever sits

on. A child, her mother, both struck
with panic moments after the first pop.

There's something surreal about being
shot at. How the snap of gunfire

pauses you. Then the rush of blood,
like an electric shock, to the brain. Horror

& elation of being alive. Soon crucifixes
& candles will drape this corner

like a hand-me-down blanket. Of course,
no one seen nothing. Only the sound

of lead wedged in a young man's back.
After the neighbors, the cops will

interrogate the liquor store security
video across the street. This chore

of solving the crime, like trying to piece
together a jigsaw puzzle, blank side up.

## Busted Lullaby

lull of determined
thumps against his head & back
again & again

again lull again
head thumps & determined his
against of & back

back again against
thumps of & lull & his head
determined again

## 3 Little Pigs

Me & uncle in a car when a police pulls us over yelling aiming his gun at
uncle's head when second police comes with more sirens & fear & get
down on the floor uncle tells me & don't move & I don't when the first
police pulls uncle out pushes to the street & slugs his head *POW!* his
back *CLUNK!* when third police arrives & now 2 police aiming 1 police
spraying & 1 uncle with fire in his eyes with snot from his nose when
at last a police lowers his gun says wait that's not the guy sorry amigo
& they all leave.

# Police Dog

it's all just
play      to wrap

your mouth
around a man's

wrist      barely
break skin

to growl      tug
hold on till

the officers
arrive      only then

do things
get serious




# Night

The air is like gunmetal.
                              An explosion
of music rattles a van's shell as it waits

the stoplight. I cross the street
and my breath rises
                              blends into the night

like a car alarm.
                              A man clutches frozen
towels and a tip box outside CITGO's car wash.

His face—scarf-smothered
                              ninja-style
as if seeing and breathing were done with

the eyes alone.
                    The clerk inside looks
vulnerable until I spot mounted cameras.

What else—pistol?  Baseball bat?
Something defensive
                    deadly

tucked under the counter.
                    I continue
home in skin not safe to be at night.



## Want

As July overwhelms the city
like a drunk lover & the shade

offers nothing but an illusion
of cool, a cluster of sun-whipped

men leans against brick that looks
more chewed up steak than wall.

They want work & wait here
in the hot for an offer. One man

wipes sweat from above
his lip while another sits still

as death. An oil-pissing truck
staggers by & stops—waves

of heat rise from the hood
as a faded-green sleeve hangs

out the window & summons
three men standing to the side.

After they leap onto the bed
like Olympic athletes, the truck

farts & pulls away to its next job.
A man left behind tilts his head up

as if ready for the sky to burst
& soil everything with water.


## Bones

Your feet are a slow train
wreck of cuneiforms
      & metatarsals fallen off

    track. Too many overtimes
standing, bagging melon & meat
      frozen peas & six-packs wedged

    careful against egg cartons
loafs of bread
      tomatoes that piss if touched

    too hard. At home you stand
at the sink full of yesterday's
      plates sauce-caked pots

    butter knives tough
with peanut butter.
      Tonight you fall

    asleep in a chair trying
to ignore the 52 bones of your feet
      each one humming its own pain.

# While Late Capitalism

[Crammd-in-&-bangin-against-each-othr-in-a-dark-aluminm-box-mostly-
women-severl-childrn-&-some-infants-fuss-an-assuring-sound-in-this-
lack-of-oxygen-they-say-drops-em-like-fleas-or-like-th-man-who-died-
standin-6-hrs-into-th-trip-more-nuisance-than-grief-since-no-one-in-th-
truck-knew-him-a-woman-kind-enough-draped-her-limp-babys-serape-
over-th-mans-head-which-nods-back-&-frth-with-each-bump-in-th-road-
thank-god-th-corpses-dont-smell-but-th-hot-piss-stink-is-making-bodies-
vomit-on-bodies-stuffd-next-to-them-must-feel-like-days-since-th-coyote-
lockd-th-trailer-door-&-theres-little-struggle-now-except-a-woman-
trying-to-scratch-a-hole-thru-th-rig-wall-as-she-prays-some-phrase-or-
word-some-idea-that-doesnt-translate-well-in-Englsh]

# Nightshift

After the rake & shovel,
after the sun & dirt, he pulls on
his botas, clasps his *Durango*

belt buckle. It's Saturday
night & the pearls of his red
collared shirt are snapped

& ready for the San Louis—
restaurant turned discotheque
by evening. Two shots

of whiskey get things going,
twenty-five cent bottles
of Old Style buzz the rest

of the night. After the chairs
& tables are pushed against
the wall, the Mexican sextet

begins, and the stepping
& twirling carves thru the thick
of cigarette smoke & musk.

One woman's toes are stuffed
like gravel into size-six
heels, blemishes concealed

by Swap N' Shop stockings.
In the dim light she doesn't
notice the dirt & scars

embedded into the hands
that hold her close while she
flitters to the music

and sweeps the tiled floor
dancing fast, then slow,
then fast again.

Lidia Torres

## Three Keys

I inherit three skeleton keys,
a thick metal ring
tied in a bow at the end.

These keys cannot lock
the bare rooms with quiet
ghosts of three brothers.

I call them at night,
the rusted metal ringing
in my pocket. My brother answers, tapping

the conga skin with the tips of his fingers,
lightly, not to wake my sister
in the room next door dreaming

of my father. In her dreams,
he is counting beds, readying rooms.
Another brother taps the clave's beat.

The last brother answers by barely scraping
a güiro. Then we are all
in the same dream, alive and dead.

There is the palm tree you wanted.
The mangos are so low,
they graze your fingers

when you try to reach them.
Limes among roses, orchids.
Even the roots bear fruit

in our garden. The scent
of guavas. The tapping
and scraping of the trío.

## Visiting the Dead

My father woke up,
shrugged off the soil
and headed for the garden.
A ghost in a suit poking beans,
prodding plantains and tomatoes.
He smiled, that rare twist
of the lips, and patted
the bare edges of his sons' graves.
They rested as he paced
among the tubers.

Later that day it was sancocho
for supper. I peeled
and chopped the tubers, chanting
yuca, ñame, yautía, batata.
The fragrance of cilantro settled
over the vacant table.
How the one bottomless pot once
served my father, my brothers
and the living. The heat
stroked my face as I leaned
over the green bananas softening,
clinging to the roots.

## Listening for Her

I clean my mother's body
abandoned long ago by its brain cells.

She allows me to move her limbs,
unfold her skin, yielding

like an infant. Prying into the deepest
places, she cooperates sensing that

this is good. The body does
what it must then we are left

to clean up. Work that she no longer
comprehends. As I wrap the diaper

around her waist, I feel her
lumpy belly, first home

to ten children she patiently
cleaned and wrapped.

My reflection meets hers.
'Scucha, she says.

And I listen and listen
gazing into the mirror with her.

Listening as I did at fourteen,
five sisters in one room.

Our legs outgrowing the bedframe.
Escucha, we would say in the dark,

as she shuffled past the door.

## Two Guavas

*Vega Baja, Puerto Rico*

They rested in the car
scenting the drive to Ponce.
Two pale yellow fruits
plucked from the source:
the tree in my aunt's garden
surrounded by orchids growing

out of coconut shells
and plantains hiding their tender fruit.
Nanda crushed the juicy pink
pulp with sugar and ice.
While we sipped the limber,
a bird sucked the nectar
of a guava from the tree.
That night, we slept
with their fragrance
ripening in the dark.

## A Weakness for Boleros

The bolero was composed for you and me.
For all the ten year olds drawn
to the plastic dials of the radio,
drooling a bit perhaps,
swaying uncontrollably as the air
in the room tensed, focused
on the sweet vortex of the singer's voice.
Our breath caught between
the violin strings and the keys
of the piano, the soft beating
of the cowbell in the shadows of the song.
What did I know of that word *querer*
as I slow danced with a clutched album cover?
In another part of the city, you listened
and rocked in place. Both of us dazed
as the voice lifted us.

# Daphne as a Drum

*pa' Juan*

In a clearing, the percussionist pauses
noticing the dark hips
in a tree's shape.

He puts his arms around
the curve of its waist and holds on,
ear pressed to the trunk.

He strokes the bark
with calloused hands.
Daphne aches inside

her home. She wants to bend
and let down her hair when his palms
brush her stiff back and behind.

He whispers, you are red
inside, full of music.
So he fells the tree,

rhythms thudding, echoing
from the fallen trunk.
Slowly, delicately, he scoops out

everything, the sap
sticking to his fingers
And when it is over

her figure remains in the wooden
contours, waist and hips
responding below the taut skin

he taps between his legs.

# Spirit Boat

*for Arden*

*Park Slope and El Albayzín*

The jasmine bloomed all summer,
sprouting delicate white
flowers that fade to purple
in each corner of the room.
The flowers fell into the black frame
after scenting the room,
a cargo of preserved moments.

In my little flat in Granada
I unfolded the letters,
hung them outside my window
with the laundry, glanced
at the photograph of the boat.
The wooden pins clattered
down in the courtyard.
Then supper: a solitary salad,
a quart of beer, a large melon.
Bad salsa on the radio.
In the morning, the jeans
were stiff, still damp
from the moonlight.

The letters traveled
in the spirit boat, made their way
from Long Island to Spain,
drifted in the Mediterranean,
settled in Brooklyn.

## Adrift

Nights, I would go swimming
in the deserted pool
of the community college.
Nights of the clean drift,
occasionally diving to touch
the tiles below. Then reaching
for that solitary buoyancy
until the lights went out,
the closing signal.
Afterwards, the lifeguard and I
stripped and yelled to each other
from separate changing rooms.
Our voices carried over the nearby pool.
Going to the showers, we glimpsed
each other's bodies. His modest
shrunken penis, my forgotten breasts.
I was 22. I knew nothing of this
body's cravings as we showered,
touching our curves, scars,
and shouted over the water, kicking
the bar of soap between the stalls.

## Poema en un carro público

*Brooklyn, Oct. 1998*

The cab driver hears sympathy
in our Spanish, recognizes
your hat. ¿Españoles? No, poetas.
"Write something for her," he says.
"To bring us back together."
If only the page would flower
on its own. I look at the trees.
Los árboles perdieron sus hojas
porque no pude estar contigo.

Suddenly, I don't care
about his wife or the driver
enjoying our argument over grammar.
You are in the present. I favor the future.
Future perfect. Perfect traffic
cooperating while we write
three four-line stanzas.
The buildings without light,
the obligatory horizon,
the return of the trees now in bloom.
He thinks we are husband and wife.
Wedded in the back seat for an instant,
we race to finish before the bridge.
We barely feel the pavement
as we leave the car and embrace.
The driver pulls away with his poem.
I have the lines we left out.

## Blackout

*New York City, August 13, 2003*

All this
is not unusual in DR or Iraq.
The city's extension cord shorts.
Afternoon, offices evacuate.
The focus is on feet,
some people walking through boroughs
for the first time. We stare at our feet,
elbow to elbow eyeing packed buses.
Some hitch rides on the back
of trucks. An orderly mob of feet,
legs pushing past fearless
grocery stores. Lincoln
center, Harlem, finally

in Washington Heights the street
party has begun. Batteries boost
the curbside music, click of candlelit
dominoes, night meeting a stream
of car lights, congestion
of bodies. Everyone is polite and briefly
romantic in the dark. On my block,
there's a woman selling hot pasteles
on paper plates, with ketchup
if you want.

# About the Contributors

**Rosa Alcalá** is currently an assistant professor in the Bilingual Creative Writing Department at the University of Texas at El Paso. She has published her poems in a variety of literary magazines, including *The Kenyon Review, Bombay Gin, P-Queue, Chain, Mandorla, XCP (Cross Cultural Poetics), Open City,* and *A.BACUS.* A selection of her work also appeared in *Some Maritime Disasters this Century* (Belladonna Books, 2003), and *Cinturones de óxido: de Buffalo con amor/Rust Belt Encounters: From Buffalo with Love,* translated by Ernesto Livón-Grosman and Omar Pérez (Torre de Letras, La Habana, Cuba, 2005). An accomplished translator of poetry, her translation of Lourdes Vázquez's *Bestiary* was published by Bilingual Press in 2003. Alcalá has also published translations of Cecilia Vicuña, including *El Templo* (Situations Press, 2001), *Cloud-net* (Art in General, 1999), and the poem-essay "Ubixic del Decir, 'Its Being Said': A Reading of a Reading of the Popol Vuh," published in *With Their Hands and Their Eyes: Maya Textiles, Mirrors of a Worldview* (Etnografish Museum, Belgium, 2003). Alcalá received an MFA in creative writing from Brown University, and a PhD in English from the State University of New York at Buffalo.

**Francisco Aragón** (Editor) is the author of *Puerta del Sol* (Bilingual Press, 2005). His anthology publications include *Inventions of Farewell: A Book of Elegies* (W. W. Norton), *Under the Fifth Sun: Latino Literature from California* (Heyday Books), *American Diaspora: Poetry of Displacement* (University of Iowa Press), *How to Be This Man* (Swan Scythe Press), and *Bend, Don't Shatter* (Soft Skull Press). He is also the author of three limited-edition chapbooks. His poems and translations have appeared in various print and Web publications, including *Chain, Chelsea, Crab Orchard Review, Electronic Poetry Review, Jacket, Puerto del Sol,* and *ZYZZYVA.* He is currently Director of Letras Latinas—the literary unit of the Institute for Latino Studies at the University of Notre Dame. A native of San Francisco and long-time resident of Spain, he resides in South Bend, Indiana. Visit his Web site at www.franciscoaragon.net.

**Naomi Ayala** works as an education consultant, freelance writer, and teacher, and is a Visiting Humanities Scholar for *Hermana a Hermana/Sister to Sister.* Her poems and book reviews have most recently appeared in *Ploughshares, Poetry Daily, Saranac Review, Hostos Review/Revista Hostoniana, MARGIN: Exploring Modern Magical Realism, Saheb Ghalam Daily*

(Afghanistan), *Gargoyle, Tiger Tail, Feminist Teacher, The Washington Post*, and the *New Hampshire Review*. Her poetry has recently been anthologized in *Boriquén to Diasporican: Puerto Rican Poetry from Aboriginal Times to the New Millennium* (University of Wisconsin Press, 2005) and *Latino Boom: An Anthology of U.S. Latino Literature* (Longman, 2006).

**Richard Blanco** was made in Cuba, assembled in Spain, and imported to the United States—meaning his mother, seven months pregnant, and the rest of the family arrived as exiles from Cuba to Madrid, where he was born. Forty-five days later, the family emigrated once more and settled in Miami, where he was raised and educated. Since 1999, Blanco has traveled extensively and has lived in several places, including Guatemala; Brazil; Connecticut, where he was assistant professor of creative writing and Latino Literature; and Washington, DC, where he taught at Georgetown University and American University. His first book of poetry, *City of a Hundred Fires*, explores the yearnings and negotiation of cultural identity as a Cuban-American, and received the Agnes Lynch Starrett Poetry Prize from the University of Pittsburgh Press (1998). His second book, *Directions to The Beach of the Dead* (University of Arizona Press, 2005) further explores the themes of home and place. His poems have appeared in *The Best American Poetry 2000* and *Great American Prose Poems*, and have been featured on National Public Radio's *All Things Considered*. A builder of bridges and poems, Blanco earned both a BS in civil engineering and an MFA in creative writing (1997). He currently lives in Miami, where he writes and works as a consultant engineer.

**Brenda Cárdenas's** chapbook of poetry *From the Tongues of Brick and Stone* was published by Momotombo Press in 2005. She also co-edited and contributed to *Between the Heart and the Land: Latina Poets in the Midwest* (MARCH/Abrazo Press, 2001). Her work has appeared in a varied range of publications, including *Poetic Voices without Borders, U.S. Latino Literature Today, Prairie Schooner, RATTLE, Bum Rush the Page: A Def Poetry Jam, Learning by Heart: Contemporary American Poetry about School*, and *Under the Pomegranate Tree: The Best New Latino Erotica*, among others. With *Sondio Ink (quieto)*, a spoken word and music ensemble, she co-produced and released the CD *Chicano, Illinoize: The Blue Island Sessions*, in 2001. Among her honors are two Illinois Arts Council finalist awards. She holds an MFA in creative writing from the University of Michigan, Ann Arbor. She currently teaches at Milwaukee Area Technical College in Wisconsin.

**Albino Carrillo** is a native New Mexican poet whose work has appeared in many literary journals, including *The Americas Review, South Dakota Review, Antioch Review, Blue Mesa Review, Puerto del Sol*, and *Columbia: A*

*Journal of Literature and Art.* He has new poems forthcoming in *World Order Magazine*, edited by Herbert Woodward Martin. His book, *In the City of Smoking Mirrors*, was published by the University of Arizona Press in 2004. Carrillo professes poetry and creative writing at the University of Dayton, a Catholic, comprehensive university in the Marianist tradition.

**Steven Cordova** is the author of the poetry chapbook *Slow Dissolve* (Momotombo Press, 2003). A native of San Antonio, he has published poems in *Art & Understanding, The James White Review, Evergreen Chronicles, Borderlands: Texas Poetry Review, Barrow Street, The Journal, Callaloo, Northwest Review,* and the online journals *La Petite Zine, The Cortland Review,* and *Lodestar Quarterly.* His work has also appeared in the anthology *Ravishing DisUnities: Real Ghazals in English* (Wesleyan University Press, 2000), edited by the late Agha Shahid Ali. He holds a degree from the University of Texas in Austin and lives and works in New York City.

**Eduardo C. Corral** holds degrees from Arizona State University and the Iowa Writers' Workshop. His poems have appeared in *Black Warrior Review, Colorado Review, Indiana Review, Meridian, The Nation, Poetry Northwest,* and *Quarterly West.* His work has been honored with a "Discovery"/*The Nation* award and a MacDowell Colony residency.

**David Dominguez** is the author of *Work Done Right* (University of Arizona Press, 2003). An earlier collection, *Marcoli Sausage,* appeared in 2000 as part of Gary Soto's Chicano Chapbook Series. A native of Fresno, his poems have appeared in various publications, including *El Andar, Bloomsbury Review, Crab Orchard Review, Faultline, Flies, Cockroaches and Poets,* and *Solo.* His work was also featured in the anthology *How Much Earth: The Fresno Poets* (Heyday Books) as well as on the Web at *Poetry Daily.* He holds degrees from the University of California at Irvine and the University of Arizona, where he completed his MFA in creative writing. He currently teaches writing and literature at Reedley College in California.

**John Olivares Espinoza** is the author of *Gardens of Eden* (Chicano Chapbook Series) and *Aluminum Times,* winner of the Swan Scythe Press poetry prize. His work has appeared in various journals, including *Quarterly West, Rivendell, Poetry International,* and *El Andar,* which awarded him their annual Prize for Literary Excellence in poetry. His work has also been anthologized in *Under the Fifth Sun: Latino Literature from California* (Heyday Books) and *How to Be This Man* (Swan Scythe Press). A Soros Fellow and former Pushcart Prize nominee, Espinoza holds degrees from the University of California at Riverside, and Arizona State University, where he completed an MFA in creative writing. He currently teaches writing and literature at the National Hispanic University in San Jose, California.

**Gina Franco** is the author of *The Keepsake Storm* (University of Arizona Press, 2004). Her poems have appeared in *The Black Warrior Review, Crazyhorse, The Georgia Review, Mosaic, Prairie Schooner, Seneca Review, Fence Magazine*, and elsewhere. She holds an MFA from Cornell University and is a PhD candidate at Cornell, as well. Her honors include runner up for the 2002 Kathryn A. Morton Prize in Poetry with Sarabande Books and Special Mention in the 2005 Pushcart Prize Anthology. She currently teaches at Knox College in Galesburg, Illinois, where she is an assistant professor. She is at work on a collection of poems, *Mother Lode*, about copper-mining in Arizona.

**Venessa Maria Engel-Fuentes's** poetry was featured in *Between the Heart and the Land/Entre el corazón y la tierra: Latina Poets in the Midwest* (MARCH/Abrazo Press, 2001). Her work has also appeared in *Swerve* magazine, and she was a 2003 SASE/Jerome grant recipient. She has led several writing workshops for young children. She holds a BA from Macalester College in Women's and Gender Studies. She is currently the Coordinator of Youth Programs at the Loft Literary Center in Minneapolis, Minnesota, where she lives with her son.

**Kevin A. González** was born in San Juan, Puerto Rico, in 1981. He holds degrees from Carnegie Mellon University and the University of Wisconsin–Madison, where he was a Martha Meier Renk Poetry Fellow. His poems have appeared in *Poetry, McSweeney's, Callaloo, El Nuevo Día*, and *The Progressive*; and his stories have appeared in *Playboy, Indiana Review*, and *Virginia Quarterly Review*, as well as in the *Best New American Voices* anthology. Currently, he is a graduate fellow at the Iowa Writers' Workshop.

**David Hernandez's** poetry collections include *Always Danger* (Southern Illinois University Press, 2006), winner of the Crab Orchard Award Series in Poetry, and *A House Waiting for Music* (Tupelo Press, 2003). His poems have appeared in *The Missouri Review, Ploughshares, FIELD, TriQuarterly, AGNI, The Southern Review*, and *The Iowa Review*. He is a recipient of a grant from the Ludwig Vogelstein Foundation, and his drawings have also appeared in literary magazines, including a feature in *Indiana Review*. David lives in Long Beach, California, and is married to writer Lisa Glatt. Visit his Web site at www.DavidAHernandez.com.

**Scott Inguito** was born in Santa Maria, California, and lives in San Francisco. He received a BA in English from San Francisco State University and an MFA in poetry from the Iowa Writers' Workshop. His poems and visual art have appeared in various magazines including *Fence, Aufgabe, el pobre mouse, 1913: a journal of forms*, and *Dánta*. He is the author of the chapbook *lection* (Subday Press 2006). He currently teaches at Notre Dame de Namur University, Belmont, California.

**Sheryl Luna** is the inaugural winner of the Andrés Montoya Poetry Prize, awarded in 2004 by the Institute for Latino Studies at the University of Notre Dame. This national prize honors a first book by a Latino/a poet. Her collection, *Pity the Drowned Horses*, was published by University of Notre Dame Press in 2005. She has been a finalist for the National Poetry Series book awards and has published her work in such journals as *The Georgia Review, Prairie Schooner, Borderlands: Texas Poetry Review, Poetry Northwest, The Amherst Review, Puerto del Sol*, and *Kalliope: A Journal of Women's Art and Literature*. A native of El Paso, she holds a PhD from the University of North Texas.

**Carl Marcum** is the author of *Cue Lazarus* (University of Arizona Press, 2001), a 2nd Place Co-Winner for Best Poetry in 2002 for the Latino Literary Hall of Fame Awards. He is also the author of *El Medio Reza* (The Chicano Chapbook Series). His poems have appeared in various journals, including *Blue Mesa Review, Shades of December*, and *The Lucid Stone*, among others. His honors include a fellowship from the National Endowment for the Arts, a Wallace Stegner Fellowship from Stanford University and the D.H. Lawrence Fellowship from the University of New Mexico's Taos Summer Writers' Conference. A native of Arizona, he currently resides in Chicago and teaches creative writing and literature at DePaul University.

**María Meléndez** is the author of *How Long She'll Last in This World* (University of Arizona Press, 2006). While completing graduate studies in creative writing at the University of California, Davis, she served as area coordinator for California Poets in the School. In 2000, she was awarded and Artists-in-Communities grant from the California Arts Council to support her work as writer-in-residence at the UC Davis Arboretum, where she taught environmental poetry workshops for the public. She has authored one chapbook of poetry, *Base Pairs*, and edited two anthologies, *Nest of Freedom* and *Moon Won't Leave Me Alone*. She also serves as associate editor for Momotombo Press, and her poetry, articles, and short fiction appear in a number of magazines, such as *Puerto del Sol* and *International Quarterly*.

**Carolina Monsivais** is a recipient of the Premio Poesía Tejana for her book, *Somewhere Between Houston and El Paso: Testimonies of a Poet* (Wings Press, 2001). Monsivais worked with survivors of domestic violence/sexual assault in Texas and New Mexico. A dedicated advocate/activist in the field of violence against women and children, she co-founded

The Women Writers' Collective (WWC). The WWC, a community-based group of women writers and activists, showcases the talents of women writers and artists while raising awareness for issues related to women and allies in the community. The WWC has held readings to raise funds and awareness for Amigos de las Mujeres de Juárez and has co-sponsored events to raise awareness through the arts with Border Senses and the El Paso Center against Family Violence. She has also volunteered with Nuestra Palabra: Latino Writers Having Their Say, a non-profit organization that primarily promotes literature by Latinas/os and writers of color. Her poetry has appeared in several literary journals and *U.S. Latino Literature Today.* Currently, she is working on her MFA in creative writing at New Mexico State University. She resides in Santa Teresa, New Mexico, near her hometown, El Paso, Texas.

**Adela Najarro** holds a doctorate in literature and creative writing from Western Michigan University, as well as an MFA from Vermont College. She currently teaches at Cabrillo College as part of the Puente Project, a program designed to support Latinidad in all its aspects, while preparing community college students to transfer to four-year colleges and universities. Her extended family's emigration from Nicaragua to San Francisco began in the 1940s and concluded in the eighties when the last of the family settled in the Los Angeles area. She has published poems in numerous journals, including *Notre Dame Review, Nimrod International Journal of Poetry & Prose, Blue Mesa Review, Crab Orchard Review, ACM: Another Chicago Magazine, Artful Dodge,* and *Cimarron Review.*

**Urayoán Noel** was born in San Juan, Puerto Rico, in 1976, and has lived in New York City since 1999. He is the author of the books of poetry *Kool Logic/La lógica kool* (Bilingual Press, 2005) and *Boringkén* (Ediciones Vértigo, 2006), and (with composer Monxo López) of the poetry/rock/performance DVD *Kool Logic Sessions: Poems, Pop Songs, Laugh Tracts.* His self-published, post-industrial book of poems *Las flores del mall* (2000, 2003) has been called "delicious and infamous," and is a prized cult artifact of the new Puerto Rican poetry. He has published translations of Latin American and Latino poets, including Cecilia Vicuña, Nancy Mercado, Fernanda Laguna, and Edwin Torres. He is a doctoral student in Spanish at New York University and vocalist for the rock band *objet petit a.* He lives on the Grand Concourse, near Yankee Stadium.

**Deborah Parédez** is the author of the poetry collection, *This Side of Skin* (Wings Press, 2002). Her work has appeared in various anthologies, including *Daughters of the Fifth Sun: A Collection of U.S. Latina Fiction and Poetry*

(Putman, 1995), *This Promiscuous Light* (Wings Press, 1996), and *¡Flori-canto Sí!: A Collection of Latina Poetry* (Penguin, 1998), as well as various literary journals. A native of San Antonio, she has lived in Seattle, Chicago, and New York City. She currently teaches in the theater department at the University of Texas in Austin and is at work on a book about Selena.

**Emmy Pérez** grew up in Santa Ana, California. A graduate of Columbia University's MFA program and the University of Southern California, she has received poetry fellowships from the New York Foundation for the Arts and the Fine Arts Work Center in Provincetown. She is the author of a poetry chapbook, *Solstice* (Swan Scythe Press, 2003). Her poems have appeared or are forthcoming in *Prairie Schooner, Indiana Review, North American Review, New York Quarterly, LUNA, Crab Orchard Review, Notre Dame Review, Borderlands: Texas Poetry Review, Karavan* (translated into Swedish), and other publications. Her fiction has appeared in *Story* and *Blue Mesa Review*, and she received the James D. Phelan Award for her prose writing. As a writing teacher, she has worked with women prison inmates, adult literacy students, youth in a juvenile detention center, and college students (most recently as a visiting assistant professor of creative writing at the University of Texas at El Paso). She is a member of the Women Writers' Collective in El Paso and directs a spoken word poetry project for under-served youth with BorderSenses.

**Paul Martínez Pompa** received his BA in English from the University of Chicago and his MFA in creative writing from Indiana University, where he also served as a poetry editor for the *Indiana Review*. His chapbook, *Pepper Spray*, was published by Momotombo Press in 2006. He currently teaches composition and creative writing at Triton College in River Grove, Illinois. He lives with his wife in Chicago.

**Lidia Torres** is the author of *A Weakness for Boleros* (Mayapple Press, 2005). She received a poetry fellowship from the New York Foundation for the Arts, and her poems have appeared in *Massachusetts Review, Bilingual Review/Revista Bilingüe, Hayden's Ferry Review, Calabash, Ploughshares*, and the *Beacon Best of 2000*. She lives in New York City, where she works with inner-city students in an academic intervention program.

# Further Reading

A selection of recommended books by poets who were eligible for inclusion in *The Wind Shifts* but who, for reasons mentioned in the preface, were not in the final selection include the following:

*Bent to the Earth* (Carnegie Mellon University Press, 2005)
　　by Blas Manuel de Luna
*A Book Called Rats* (Lynx House Press, 2003)
　　by Miguel Murphy
*Bus Stop and Other Poems* (Calaca Press, 1998)
　　by Manuel J. Vélez
*A Question of Gravity and Light* (University of Arizona Press, 2007)
　　by Blas Falconer
*Death of a Mexican* (Bear Star Press, 2007)
　　by Manuel Paul Lopez
*How to Undress a Cop* (Arte Público Press, 2000)
　　by Sarah Cortez
*Lucky Wreck* (Autumn House Press, 2006)
　　by Ada Limón
*mahcic* (Calaca Press, 2005)
　　by Tómas Riley
*My Sweet Unconditional* (Tía Chucha Press, 2006)
　　by Ariel Robello
*Counter Daemons* (Litmus Press, 2006)
　　by Roberto Harrison
*The Outer Bands* (University of Notre Dame Press, 2007)
　　by Gabriel Gomez
*Ruin* (Alice James Books, 2006)
　　by Cynthia Cruz
*Other Fugitives and Other Strangers* (Tupelo Press, 2006)
　　by Rigoberto González
*Skin Tax* (Heyday Books, 2004)
　　by Tim Z. Hernandez

A number of Latino and Latina poets whose fine work has appeared in various literary journals and chapbooks include: William Archila, Carmen Calatayud, Diana Marie Delgado, Suzanne Ocampo-Frischkorn, Angela Garcia, José B. Gonzalez, Octavio R. Gonzalez, Javier Huerta, Martin Lemos, Raina J. León, Pablo Miguel Martínez, Kristin Naca, Victor Olivares, Marisela Treviño Orta, Ruben Quesada, Peter Ramos, Verónica Reyes, Jorge Sánchez, Renee Soto, and Roberto Tejada.

# Acknowledgments

A project of this magnitude involves the collaboration and support of a number of people. First and foremost a sincere thanks to the poets for saying *Yes*, and for their patience and professionalism throughout the process. Working with them made tangible the oftentimes intangible expression, "community of writers." A word of thanks to colleagues near and far who offered relevant thoughts on poetry and poetry editing in particular, as well as words of encouragement. A number are mentioned in the preface for putting certain poets on my radar. They are Rigoberto González, Emmy Pérez, Richard Yañez, and Valerie Sayers. To these names, I'd like to add Rane Arroyo, Patti Hartmann, Jack Hicks, Valerie Martínez, John Matthias, Orlando Ricardo Menes, María Meléndez, and Bryce Milligan. This project was a natural outgrowth of my work as director of Letras Latinas, the literary program at the Institute for Latino Studies (ILS) at Notre Dame. The Institute has provided a home since 2003, and I am very proud to be a part of it. I would like to thank Gil Cárdenas for bringing me on board and providing a relevant context from which to work. Thanks, as well, to ILS colleagues Caroline Domingo, Doug Franson, and Tim Ready, for their support and friendship. Cristina Gutierrez, my editorial assistant, was crucial in assembling this manuscript. On a more personal note, I'd like to thank a few people who, from a distance, continued to offer indelible support and the gift of their friendship: George Castillo, John Chendo, Jim McElroy, and Steve McCarthy. And finally, a word of thanks to my family—my brother Tomás, my sister Martha, my brother-in-law Kurt, my niece Angela, and my nephews Garrick, Trevor, Tomasito, and Luis, for being an anchor from the San Francisco/Bay Area.

# Source Notes

The editor would like to thank and acknowledge the publishers and editors of presses and journals who gave many of the poems in this anthology (at times in earlier versions) their first readers.

The epigraph at the beginning of *The Wind Shifts* is from *Borderlands/La Frontera: The New Mestiza.* Copyright © 1987, 1999 by Gloria Anzaldúa. Reprinted by permission of Aunt Lute Books.

**Rosa Alcalá** "Cante Grande" and "The Silversmith's Wife & the Chestnut Vendor" appeared in *Rebel Road: Poems in the Garden I & II* (New York: Situations Press, 2001). "The Silversmith's Wife & the Chestnut Vendor" also appeared in translation in the anthology, *Cinturones de óxido: de Buffalo con amor/Rust Belt Encounters: From Buffalo with Love,* translated by Ernesto Livón-Grossman y Omar Pérez (Torres de Letras, La Habana, Cuba, 2005). "Migration" appeared in *Mandorla* #8. "The Sixth Avenue Go-Go Lounge," and "Patria" are reprinted by permission of the author.

**Francisco Aragón** "Café Central," "Lunch Break," and "Bridge Over Strawberry Creek" are from *Puerta del Sol,* by Francisco Aragón, published by Bilingual Press. Copyright © 2005. "Poem with Citations from the OED" appeared in *Electronic Poetry Review.* "Al Viejo Mundo" appeared in *Crab Orchard Review.* "Portrait with Lines of Montale" appeared in *The Chattahoochee Review.* "Ernesto Cardenal in Berkeley," "Grid," "Far Away," and "Al Viejo Mundo" are reprinted by permission of the author.

**Naomi Ayala** "Papo, Who'd Wanted to Be an Artist," "It Was Late and She Was Climbing," "This Breathless Minute," "My Brother Pito," "For 'S'" are from *Wild Animals on the Moon,* by Naomi Ayala (Curbstone Press, 1997). Reprinted with permission of Curbstone Press, distributed by Consortium. "Hole" appeared in *Ploughshares* (Spring 2005). "Within Me," "Thus," "Griot," and "Horses" are reprinted by permission of the author. "Within Me" was translated from the Spanish by the author and Francisco X. Stork. "Thus" was translated from the Spanish by the author.

**Richard Blanco** "Mother Picking Produce," "Shaving," and "Varadero en Alba" from *City of a Hundred Fires,* by Richard Blanco. Copyright © 1998. Reprinted by permission of the University of Pittsburgh Press. "Chilo's Daughters Sing for Me in Cuba," "What Is Not Mine," "Mexican Almuerzo in New England," "Time as Art in The Eternal City," "In Defense of Livorno," and "Somewhere to Paris" are from *Directions to The Beach of the Dead,* by Richard Blanco, published by the University of Arizona Press. Copyright © 2005.

**Brenda Cárdenas** "Empty Spaces," "Report from the Temple of Confessions in Old Chicano English," "Cartoon Coyote Goes Po-Mo," "*from* Sound Waves: A Series,"

"Medicine," and "Our Language" are from *From the Tongues of Brick and Stone*, by Brenda Cárdenas, published by Momotombo Press. Copyright © 2005. "Song" is printed by permission of the author.

**Albino Carrillo** "De las Mujeres Tristes," "Animal Time," "La Invención del Televisor Según Huitzilopochtli," and "H. Writes His Dead Amigos for the Sake of Clarity" are from *In the City of Smoking Mirrors*, by Albino Carrillo, published by the University of Arizona Press. Copyright © 2004. "Lament for the chilero from Las Cruces" is from *New Century Calendar* (work-in-progress) and printed by permission of the author.

**Steven Cordova** "Sissy Boy," "Across a Table," "In Your Defense," "Of Sorts," "At the Delacourt," and "Driving toward Lake Superior" are from *Slow Dissolve*, by Steven Cordova, published by Momotombo Press. Copyright © 2003. "Testing Positive" appeared in *The Cortland Review* (February 2001). "Meditations on the Jordaan" and "Daydream to You" appeared in *Diner* (Fall/Winter 2003). "Pecking Orders" appeared in *The Journal* (Autumn 1999).

**Eduardo C. Corral** "Night Gives to Things the Turning Beauty of Leaves," "Ditat Deus," "There is a Light that Never Goes Out," "Pear," "To a Mojado Who Died Crossing the Desert," "Monologue of a Vulture's Shadow," "Midnight Coffee: Rafael Rodríguez Rapún, 1936," "Julio Galan: *Misael*: Oil, Acrylic, Mixed Media on Canvas, 2001," and "Poem after Frida Kahlo's Painting *The Broken Column*" are reprinted by permission of the author.

**David Dominguez** "Pig," "Fingers," and "Mexicali" from *Work Done Right*, by David Dominguez, published by the University of Arizona Press. Copyright © 2003. "Empty Lot," "Framework," "Roof," "Chicago Title," "Cowboy," and "Elwood" are reprinted by permission of the author.

**John Olivares Espinoza** "Aching Knees in Palm Springs," "Contemporary American Hunger," "Learning Economics at Gemco," "Las Cucarachas," and "I Go Dreaming, Raking Leaves" are from *Aluminum Times*, by John Espinoza, published by Swan Scythe Press. Copyright © 2001. "Network of Bone" (originally published as "Humble Body") is from *How to Be This Man*, by John Espinoza, published by Swan Scythe Press. Copyright © 2003. "The City of Date Fruits and Bullet Wounds" appeared in *Dánta: A Poetry Journal, #2* (2003). "The Story My Grandfather Told My Mother a Few Months before His Death" reprinted by permission of the author.

**Gina Franco** "Everything Goes Down a Changeling," "Darkling," "Velvet," "These Years, in the Deepest Holes," and "The Walk Like Old Habits" are from *The Keepsake Storm*, by Gina Franco, published by the University of Arizona Press. Copyright © 2004. "The Earth Without" appeared in *The Black Warrior Review* (Vol. 30, no. 1) and is reprinted by permission of the author.

**Venessa Maria Engel-Fuentes** "Funeral" appeared in *Swerve Magazine, #1*. "Cebolla," "Como Park, 1975," "Hermanita, Hermanota," "Unit 502," "Glass Grapes," "Record-Keeping," "Pinkie," and "Insomnia" reprinted by permission of the author.